Dr. William J. Knaus is a leading authority
in Cognitive Behavioral and Rational
Emotive therapies. He is in private practice
in Longmeadow, Massachusetts. Dr. Knaus is
the author of numerous books, including *Do It Now*
and *How to Get Out of a Rut* (Prentice-Hall,
1979 and 1982).

DR. WILLIAM J. KNAUS

HOW TO CONQUER YOUR FRUSTRATIONS

Prentice-Hall, Inc., Englewood Cliffs, New Jersey 07632

Library of Congress Cataloging in Publication Data

Knaus, William J.
    How to conquer your frustrations.

    "A Spectrum Book."
    Bibliography: p.
    Includes index.
    1. Frustration.   2. Problem solving.   3. Success.
I. Title.
BF575.F7K58 1983   158'.1   83-11130
ISBN 0-13-396655-0
ISBN 0-13-396648-8 (pbk.)

1   2   3   4   5   6   7   8   9   10

ISBN 0-13-396655-0

ISBN 0-13-396648-8 {PBK.}

Editorial/production supervision by Betsy Torjussen
Cover design by Hal Siegel
Manufacturing buyer: Doreen Cavallo

This book is available at a special discount when ordered in
bulk quantities. Contact Prentice-Hall, Inc., General
Publishing Division, Special Sales, Englewood Cliffs, N.J. 07632.

Prentice-Hall International, Inc., *London*
Prentice-Hall of Australia Pty. Limited, *Sydney*
Prentice-Hall Canada Inc., *Toronto*
Prentice-Hall of India Private Limited, *New Delhi*
Prentice-Hall of Japan, Inc., *Tokyo*
Prentice-Hall of Southeast Asia Pte. Ltd., *Singapore*
Whitehall Books Limited, *Wellington, New Zealand*
Editora Prentice-Hall do Brasil Ltda., *Rio de Janeiro*

CONTENTS

LIFE FRUSTRATIONS

FOREWORDS

You're about to read an extraordinary book—one that should be on the required reading list of every literate person in the country—written by a talented and insightful psychologist, Dr. William J. Knaus. The topic, frustration, is one with which each of us has had personal, and perhaps agonizing, experience. Anyone who has ever been beset by needless anxiety and has been prevented by perceived psychological barriers from fulfilling the promise of his or her personal dignity and integrity should read this book.

This is not just another self-help book, promising quick-fix solutions to enduring problems. Nor is it a book of golden aphorisms which, if diligently memorized, produce magical lead-into-gold transformations. Instead, it's a book you're going to have to work with. You can't just sit back in your easy chair and become a mindless, passive recipient of a few witch-doctor incantations. You must be an active participant in these strategies. For, as Dr. Knaus will tell you again and again, the ultimate key to change is *action*. People involved in physical conditioning programs know the meaning of the phrase "no pain, no gain," and in this book Dr. Knaus outlines a *psychological conditioning* program that also demands that, on occasion, you're going to feel a little soreness in your psychic muscles. But even that transitory soreness comes to feel good after awhile, because it signals some good feelings—the exhilaration of personal freedom—freedom from a lot of psychological bogeymen that have prevented you from growing. In this way, the frustration tolerance training program provides you with an inoculation of low-level frustration, which then prevents you from becoming over-whelmed by intruders on your psychological life space. That is, some minor frustrations are good and help in the building of frus-tration tolerance that, in turn, add to your feeling of well-being and security. For example, if you're a procrastinator it may not be easy to make out your first "code red" list, but once you've done it, the up-beat feeling of tension reduction becomes self-reinforcing, and within a week or so you'll find yourself looking forward to listing your new priorities.

The best way to read this book is a chapter at a time. Don't try to finish it in one sitting, for the messages take time to sink in, and, more importantly, you need time to practice the actions that are involved. Take time to think about it during those off-moments—when you're folding clothes or mowing the lawn. Think of how you've been trapping and imprisoning yourself, and how, with a little effort, you can unlock the chains.

This book, although based on sound psychological principles, is not just the product of college lecture halls or laboratory exper-iments. It isn't so super-academic as to be detached from humanity. The roots of this book come firmly from the soil of Dr. Knaus's clinical practice, and its compelling message, substantiated by many illustrative case studies, is "if he or she can do it, so can I."

With Dr. Knaus's program you're not going to scale every psy-chological mountain on your first hike. He takes you on a guided tour, one step at a time, and he details *how* to take those steps. You're not going to be subjected to "glittering generalities" with built-in cop-outs, but instead you'll be trained, in almost recipelike fashion, to develop your growth potential. Dr. Knaus, to be sure, won't just take you on the easy route around those mountains, but he will, eventually, get you to the peak—and the view from the top will be well worth the climb.

RICHARD C. SPRINTHALL, Ph.D.
Director, Graduate Studies in Psychology
American International College
Springfield, Massachusetts

How to Conquer Your Frustrations is not for you if you are looking for a magical solution to eliminate your frustrations. Such magical solutions do not exist. But if you want a resource that provides a highly effective blueprint for managing frustration, you are reading the right book.

In this extraordinary book, Dr. William J. Knaus gives us a penetrating analysis of how we frustrate ourselves along with insightful strategies for how we can master our frustrations. Through his awareness-and-action approach, he shows how to master frustration, reduce stress, and feel confident.

In *How to Conquer Your Frustrations*, Dr. Knaus tackles difficult problems most psychological self-help authors fail either to recognize or to face. His materials on low frustration tolerance, for example, direct our attention to a rarely considered but highly important area of psychological concern—one that is the scaffolding for most human misery.

Dr. Knaus knowledgeably and carefully guides us through the catacombs of our frustrations to realistically experience them and helps us to develop our potential to cope with frustration.

Frustration, as Dr. Knaus clearly points out, is inevitable. We can't avoid it. Instead, we can learn how to eliminate false reasons for frustrating ourselves and how to respond effectively to legitimate frustrations. This takes time and work. But it is worth the effort when you consider the alternative—tension, stress, disorganization.

Stress researchers tell us that we make ourselves vulnerable to disease, heart trouble, and possibly cancer if we subject ourselves to ongoing distress. We may even shorten our lives. True, it takes work to improve our chances of living a longer, more satisfying life. But the work is simpler and the hours better than leading a status-quo existence where you react to change only to reduce frustration.

When you take charge of your life, you initiate changes that map a challenging course that can cause you to tap your resources. And as you learn more about your resources, as you develop confidence in your ability to face and master frustration, you find yourself.

L. RENÉ GAIENNIE, Ph.D.

Professor, School of Business Administration
University of South Florida

President, Strategic Planning Associates
Bellaire, Florida

Senior Vice-President
The Singer Company (Ret.)

PREFACE

Although almost all psychological self-help books present ways to get rid of problems and improve personal qualities and skills, few provide tested methods for dealing with the inevitable tensions and frustrations in the growth process. *How to Conquer Your Frustrations* helps fill this void.

Those who choose the pathway to self-improvement need to know how to manage their frustrations and tensions. The development of this ability constitutes a great benefit for those who want to self-improve, because frustration mastery promotes growth. In comparison, people who avoid frustrations will restrict their growth experiences, elevate their frustrations, and lead a stressful existence.

Many opportunities exist for mastering the inevitable frustrations involved in self-improvement actions, such as advancing career interests, expanding perspective, building a healthy self-concept, and contributing to the advancement of humankind. Growth also involves destroying barriers that impede progress. For example, you may want to reduce the negatives in life by losing weight, giving up smoking, overcoming shyness, persisting with plans, controlling a hot temper, getting better organized, purging a phobia, minimizing erroneous thinking, successfully challenging boredom, overriding a rut, overcoming procrastination, and so forth. In effect, by building your positive resources and destroying the barriers that block development, you can gain greater mastery over your environment and have a chance to feel fulfilled and in command.

Those who want to develop positive qualities and reduce negative habits will find that change and growth do not happen by magic. To find out what it takes to change requires getting involved in the process. To participate productively requires both willingness and the proper psychological tools. In *How to Conquer Your Frustrations* I present important frustration-management concepts that you can use imaginatively to master your frustrations.

This book has value for many other readers as well. It can serve as a resource that graduate students in counselor-training will find helpful to use in working with clients who appear resistive to change, especially those who feel insecure and doubt their ability to face the tensions and frustrations involved in growth.

In addition, learning and applying frustration-management skills can directly benefit the person who wants to work out problems in counseling. Frustration-tolerance training, as described herein, plays a pivotal role as a resource for the person who wants to make changes through counseling because frustration mastery promotes growth.

Because *How to Conquer Your Frustrations* provides both prevention and problem-intervention strategies, professors may wish to use the work as an assigned reading when they teach Psychology of Adjustment or Mental Health courses. It provides many frustration-problem-solving strategies that students can readily learn to employ to reduce stress, improve studies, and take better advantage of social and recreational opportunities.

CAN THIS BOOK SUBSTITUTE
FOR A THERAPIST?

This book will provide helpful material that you can use in your self-study. If you test and practice the written principles, you'll progress toward your goals. Indeed, some people who have read one or more of my books have written to tell me that they gained more from the books than from formal therapy. But in general I have to answer no to the question "Will the book substitute for therapy?" The book cannot interact with you in the manner of a warm, friendly, and competent therapist. You may not recognize the validity of your bibliotherapy and thus not apply some pivotal concepts. You may procrastinate if a trained specialist does not help monitor your progress. You may find it difficult to self-observe objectively. Some of your frustrations may come from concepts, ideas, images, and behaviors that seem so natural that you don't recognize or question them even when the book describes them.

THE AVAILABILITY OF THERAPY ASSISTANCE

With the exception of Rational Emotive Therapy, Behavior Therapy, and Cognitive Behavior approaches, few systems provide direct help with frustrating problems.

Most therapy systems fail to emphasize frustration tolerance and mastery as part of the therapy. Indeed, practitioners of some systems, such as classical psychoanalysis, eschew problem-solving methods, and thus prove virtually worthless for people who want to develop coping skills.

Modern psychotherapy systems, especially those oriented to Rational Emotive and Cognitive Behavior systems, have moved forward using tested multiple-treatment strategies to help people deal with frustrating problems and stresses. But even with the use of modern multiple-strategy systems, helping people master frustration takes time and *work* for both therapist and client.

Erich Fromm, a noted thinker in the psychology of love, has written that love requires care, concern, and discipline. In effect, Fromm says that love requires work. So does the development of healthy self-love. It requires caring and disciplined work to change dysfunctional frustration-creating thinking and behaving to objective thinking and functional actions.

HOW I WROTE THE BOOK

I wrote *How to Conquer Your Frustrations* to help the reader recognize, channel, and manage frustration. You can't avoid frustrations, but you do have control over how you manage them. This book suggests fresh concepts, strategies, and tactics you can use to embark upon a frustration management self-help program.

In this book I describe multiple strategies, including both awareness (cognitive) and action (behavioral) methods, for mastering frustrating circumstances. I show more than one route to get there. However, as Alfred Korzybski, the great general semanticist, noted: "the map is not the same as the territory." The map, for example, can't give you the sensory experiences of walking along one of the pathways that appear upon it. To know the territory you have to actively explore and experience it through your senses.

To get to the territory a map can help. To make a clear map of the "frustration territory," I wrote *How to Conquer Your Frustrations* in a language style called *E* prime (*E'*).

E' eliminates all forms of the verb "to be" (am, is, was, were, has been, have been, will have been). For example, instead of saying "I am a psychologist," in *E'* I would say, "I work as a psychologist." In non-*E'* I might say that "Sandra is a thief." In *E'* I would say that "Sandra stole my watch and sold it to Sam." I describe Sandra's actions (which she can learn to correct) rather than typing her as a thief. By using *E'* I can define situations, such as my functioning as a psychologist and Sandra's theft of a watch, with greater precision.

The *E'* system developed from the work of the general semanticist D. David Bourland, a follower of Alfred Korzybski. Bourland advises us to eliminate the verb "to be" because it often leads to vagueness, overgeneralizations, sloppy thinking, inaccuracies, and misleadingly abbreviated statements.

Of course, *E* prime can do little more than reduce problems caused by the inappropriate use of the verb. However, *E'* does enforce a discipline that requires the writer to express ideas in a more factual, active, and descriptive style, but it has some drawbacks. For example, in using verbatim transcripts of conversations, eliminating "to be" would change the quote. So in *How to Conquer Your Frustrations*, transcribed conversations remain as spoken. I also keep the verb when I quote other works.

I used *E'* to improve the flow of the material and to help make the message clear. Indeed, you probably will not miss the verb.

The use of the system served as a challenge to me to bring my points into sharper focus, so that you don't have to wonder what I meant and spend time interpreting my work. You can use your time working instead to manage your frustrations and developing your positive qualities.

Thanks go to the following for their suggestions during manuscript development: Fred Bliss, Richard Boss, Dr. James Brennan, Dr. Michael Cann, Dr. Ellen Casper, Frank Eldridge, Paula Eldridge, Dr. Bud Gaiennie, Dr. Nancy Haberstroh, Dr. Robert Lassiter, Eleanor Lortscher, Marsha Martin, Alan Melamed, Dr. Steven Metz, Dr. Merle Miller, Wesley Muller, David Pottenger, Richard Snyder, Dr. Richard Sprinthall, William Tuman, and Richard Weiler.

Special thanks to Mr. John Gallup, president of Strathmore Paper Company, Westfield, Massachusetts, and Mr. Charles Mulcahy, director of employee relations (Ret.) for Strathmore Paper Company, for supplying the quality paper I used for the drafting and final copy of this work.

Special thanks also go to Frank Gianfort, Lee McNamar, Jim O'Brien, and Mark Tyszka of the Xerox Store, Hartford, Connecticut, for their support, guidance, and assistance in the use of the Xerox word processing and computer equipment that I used to write this book.

I appreciate Don Martinetti's artistic contribution. Through his drawings of Gulliver, the Boy and the Golden Cape, the Time Thief, and the Wheedler, he has given us a visual treat.

Finally, I would like to acknowledge my editor, Lynne Lumsden, for her encouragement and support when I was conceptualizing *How to Conquer Your Frustrations* and Betsy Torjussen, my production editor, for her fine editorial talent and for providing valuable guidance through the final stages of manuscript development.

HOW TO CONQUER YOUR FRUSTRATIONS

PART I

THE ANATOMY
OF FRUSTRATION

Imagine the year 1789, the American Revolution, and the British General Charles Cornwallis at the battle of Yorktown surrounded by the Continental Army, fighting a siege war that he abhorred. A superior French fleet guarded the Chesapeake Bay, preventing the British fleet from entering with reinforcements and supplies. The rest we know. Cornwallis surrendered, thus ending the American Revolution.

We can easily guess how frustrated Cornwallis must have felt. His expectations that the British fleet would protect him so that he could fight the type of open warfare he preferred simply did not materialize. So at the day of surrender, the British band played "As the world turns over," reflecting their general feelings about the defeat. As for Cornwallis, he felt so frustrated by his defeat that he refused to turn his sword over to George Washington, the leader of the rag-tag Colonial Army, claiming instead that the French had defeated him.

The history books brim with tales of frustration for one and victory for another. Cornwallis's misadventure portrays but one of thousands of frustrating endings.

We all experience frustration every day of our lives. Some, like Cornwallis's great frustration, we have little control over. Most others, however, we can control.

In Part I we will look into how we contribute to the development of our own frustrations and what we can do to manage them. In this section we look closely at low frustration tolerance, because unless we can deal with our frustrations with reasonable tolerance, we will befuddle our own best interests, cause ourselves to feel emotionally distressed, and dramatically water down the quality of our daily activities.

In Chapter 1 we will consider how our frustrations tie us down and how we can start to build emotional muscle using our frustrations for a psychological workout. Chapter 2 spotlights low frustration tolerance and describes how this condition can have a disrupting effect on our emotional well-being. Chapter 3 gives us an opportunity to test our frustration tolerance and to consider ways to begin boosting it.

CHAPTER ONE

THE FRUSTRATION TRAP

In Swift's *Gulliver's Travels*, Gulliver woke up one morning and found himself tied to the ground by thousands of small threads attached the night before by tiny people called Lilliputians.

The story of Gulliver's encounter with the Lilliputians suggests a universal human experience. Many of us at times feel like Gulliver—bound by restraints and frustrations. While no one "thread" can tie us down, collectively they can. And while major life frustrations, such as the loss of a valued relationship, can prove especially frustrating, research has shown that the little frustrations of life, such as running out of clean shirts or missing the train, can accumulate and affect our physical as well as our emotional well-being.

Most people will discover as they read this book that they do a better job than they thought they did in managing their frustrations. Indeed, we should give ourselves credit for meeting the frustrating challenges in our lives. By improving our ability to tolerate and to manage the inevitable frustrations that enter our lives, we increase our chances for having more time and energy to do the things we most want to do: to build a sense of relaxed self-confidence and to feel a sense of command over the course of our lives. But if frustrations inhibit the enjoyment of sex, for example, or the ability to think clear-headedly to resolve problems alternative ways of coping need priority treatment.

In *How to Conquer Your Frustrations*, we will look into some of the mental and environmental traps that provoke our frustrations, understand how they arise, figure out how we can remove them, and eliminate both the major and the minor "Lilliputian threads" that tie down our potential. We will learn three major ways to manage frustrations:

1. *Build the body* to withstand the stress of multiple frustrations. We will review this concept in this chapter under the topic on stress.

2. *Liberate the mind* so that we can remain alert to opportunities and use our resources to take advantage of them.
3. *Change the pattern(s)* that promote needless frustrations. Don't stay stuck in a rut or repeat counterproductive actions.

While we can't always control the environment and other people, we can apply the three principles to ourselves.

However, many of our frustrations have value in that they act as motivators, impelling us to face challenges and take corrective actions. We don't want to vanquish the sensations of frustration forever (an impossible task), but rather to respond effectively to them. So first, we'll look at some examples of frustration, then define frustration, look into how frustration differs from related emotions, and discuss frustration tolerance training.

POTENTIAL FRUSTRATIONS

Frustrations come in many forms. For example, do you find yourself bogged down in your career or marriage? Do you think your future looks uneventful and uninteresting? Have you ever looked forward to a vacation trip only to have rain spoil it? Do you lose weight, then gain it back? Have you a habit, such as smoking, that you can't seem to break? Do you find it difficult to get organized, let matters slip, and helplessly watch your work pile up? Do you think some people get the breaks in life that you deserve but don't seem to get? Have you ever tried to put a simple child's toy together and found the instructions unclear and confusing? Have you ever had someone push ahead of you in line? Do people you feel close to argue with you and resist you? Do you have more than your share of unpleasant routines, such as household chores? Do you feel dissatisfied with your financial status? Has your automobile ever failed to start when you had to get to a meeting? If your life goes like that of most of us, you'll answer yes to some of these questions.

Frustrations abound—you experience them daily. Most do not present overweening problems. Some seem like glue—you feel stuck to them. Clearly, each has the capacity to elicit frustration. How you interpret the experience determines if you will *feel* frustration. As the sixth century B.C. philosopher Heraclitis noted, our eyes and ears prove poor witnesses; the mind must interpret their evidence. However, the mind can also promote frustrations based upon the meanings we give to our sensory information.

The items mentioned only scratch the surface of potential frustrations. The following frustration inventory asks you to identify some frustrating circumstances in your life.

Frustration Inventory   I designed the following twenty-item true/false test as a frustration-awareness task. Read the following statements. If you think the statement seems true or mostly true, circle the *T* next to the statement. If you think the statement seems false or mostly false, circle the *F*.

1. I feel satisfied with my career.   T   F
2. I have at least one poor habit.   T   F
3. I get to meetings on time.   T   F
4. I keep my life so well-organized that I have very little stress.   T   F
5. I don't manage my finances well.   T   F
6. I often want to get away from it all.   T   F
7. I feel frustrated when I can't find something.   T   F
8. I remain calm if I can't find a parking place.   T   F
9. I feel frustrated when I can't find something interesting to do.   T   F
10. Lateness doesn't bother me.   T   F
11. I rarely get into conflict with my neighbors.   T   F
12. When I'm stuck in traffic, I make constructive use of my time.   T   F
13. I usually get my work completed on schedule.   T   F
14. I get bugged by delayed deliveries, confusing instructions, and other matters that slow me down.   T   F
15. I get frustrated when I have to wait in line.   T   F
16. I feel tolerant of people who borrow items and don't return them.   T   F
17. I feel frustrated if I don't know the answer to a question.   T   F
18. I feel unhappy with my usual daily routine.   T   F

19. I have a quick temper.   T   F
20. I don't get bogged down by detail.   T   F

If you circled *T* for numbers 1, 3, 4, 8, 11, 12, 13, 16, and 20, and *F* for numbers 2, 5, 6, 7, 9, 10, 14, 15, 17, 18, and 19, you probably bought this book to help a friend, as you have few, if any, frustrations. Or perhaps you have not answered the questions honestly.

The inventory results may provide some clues as to whether you experience ongoing frustrations in important sectors of your life. If you answered true to any of situations 2, 5, 6, 10, 18, or 19, and false to any of situations 1, 3, 4, 11, 13, or 20, you may have identified an ongoing frustration problem worth exploring. The remaining items reflect your tolerance for normally frustrating circumstances. If you answered true to items 7, 9, 14, and 17, and false to items 8, 12, and 16, you feel frustrated by events that most people find frustrating. If you dwell upon such frustrations and regularly feel intolerant about them, you may cause yourself *double troubles*. The double-trouble principle states that you can double your frustrations when you feel frustrated about feeling frustrated!

At different times you may react to frustrations in various ways: You may see the frustration situation as a challenge, you may try to dodge the frustration, you might fight against the situation, or you may give up. At least part of your response depends upon how you perceive and define conditions so as to promote your own frustrations.

To *liberate the mind*, learn to take responsibility for creating frustrations. After all, we do not respond as robots do to electrical signals except reflexively, as when we touch a hot burner. In most cases, as the experimental psychologist Robert S. Woodword pointed out, we process what we experience, as the accompanying diagram shows.

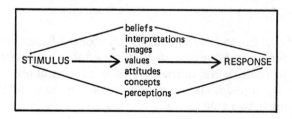

Thus, we do not mindlessly respond to most stimuli. If, for example, we get stuck in traffic, the traffic (stimulus) does not cause our response (frustration). Instead, we create our frustrations based upon what we think about the traffic. We will look into self-generated frustrations later on in this chapter when we consider how our attitudes and expectations provoke feelings of frustration.

DEFINING FRUSTRATION

Webster's Collegiate Dictionary defines frustration as "a deep chronic sense or state of insecurity and dissatisfaction arising from unresolved problems."

Frustration, a complex emotional state, erupts when we face an impediment. However, to define frustration adequately requires expanding the meaning of this concept through the use of a process definition. The following generally describes the frustration process:

1. Frustrations exist when our wants, wishes, and desires get thwarted or interrupted. The feeling results from disparities between what we want and what we find available. For example, when our level of aspiration exceeds our level of achievement we will likely experience frustration.
2. Frustrations can range from imperceptible to powerful.
3. Frustration starts from a feeling of discomfort.
4. We cause our own frustrations because of *what* and *how* we think about our impediments.
5. Strong frustrations result in mixed emotional states that have a disorganizing effect on memory and behavior.
6. Depending upon how we interpret our feelings of frustration, they can stimulate positive change, aggression, regression, complacency, or compulsive behavior.

We can expand our definition by segmenting frustration into two new categories: process and episode frustrations.

Process and Episode Frustrations   A process frustration occurs when a person continuously feels blocked in a major area of life, such as learning, work, or love. An episode frustration consists of a temporary impeding problem or condition. Almost all frustrations fall into these two categories.

8

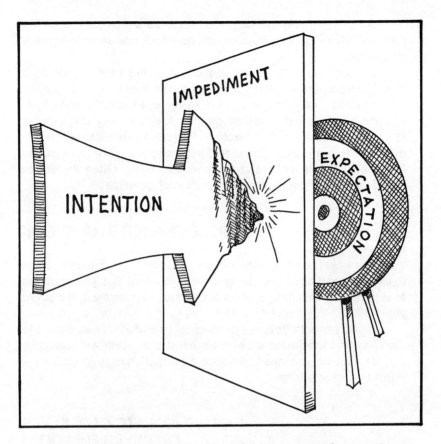

In a school situation, schoolchildren routinely experience frustrations that may prove debilitating. For example, if a child thinks she cannot master academic tasks, she could find herself entangled in an ongoing frustration from which she cannot escape except through fantasy, disruptive behavior, or apathy. She may turn to drugs. She may find herself spending time in detention at school due to her misconduct. She may burn out and demonstrate symptoms similar to adult burnout victims: sickness, depression, anxiety, lateness, and truancy.

Careers can serve as process frustrations. For example, a person who works at a job he does not like will tend to find the work routine frustrating because it represents what he does not want to do.

An unsatisfying marriage can serve as a process frustration that overflows with disappointments, boredom, and senseless power struggles.

Episode frustrations come from transient events: missing a bus, finding a part missing from a self-assembled bicycle, or putting your keys down and forgetting where you put them. Episode frustrations typically get resolved quickly and normally don't cause lingering problems. They become lingering problems when you dwell upon them to evade the real frustrations in your life. Process frustrations, however, can prove more damaging. Often we require a radical shift of perspective to break such patterns.

A RADICAL CHANGE IN OUTLOOK

You may want the body of an athlete or a model, yet avoid the effort to exercise and build your body the way you want it. If you continue to expect magical change, you will continue to frustrate and distress yourself.

If you expect effortless or magical growth, you can expect to cloud your consciousness with unrealistic or irrational concepts. To get realistic you need to adopt a radical change in outlook—effort can save effort.

CAN WE ISOLATE OURSELVES FROM FRUSTRATION?

Some process or episode frustrations can feel so uncomfortable that we want to avoid them. But in order to rid ourselves of frustrating feelings, we must also rid ourselves of all wants, wishes, and ambitions—an impossible task!

Of course, we might consider self-isolation as a solution for avoiding frustrations. But isolation can add to tensions and frustrations. For example, in sensory-deprivation studies at McGill University, research psychologist W. Heron paid students to do nothing. Although the students initially liked the idea, they all got bored and tried to find ways to amuse themselves. Few stuck with the experiment beyond twenty-four hours, despite the fact that they had originally volunteered to stay longer. Evidently, the students' attitudes about getting paid for temporarily living in isolation changed significantly as a result of the experience.

FRUSTRATION: A MATTER OF PERCEPTION

We think that situations frustrate us, but situations only have the *potential* to evoke thoughts and feelings of frustration. For example, we get a flat tire on the way to work and we think that makes us feel frustrated. The flat tire serves as the catalyst. It does not cause the frustration. The feeling of frustration arises when the flat tire prevents us from achieving our objective. For example, we may want to get to work on time *and* not have to remove and replace the flat tire. If we didn't want to get to work on time and didn't mind changing flat tires, we would not feel frustrated.

When our wants, desires, and goals get thwarted, we normally feel frustration, which reflects an *attitude* about the unwanted condition. Frustration does not get provoked by circumstances but results mainly from mental processes: our ideas about people, events, concepts, and feelings. In other words, we stir up our own frustrations based upon our interpretations and expectations of life events. As Mark Twain reputedly said: "I've had a lot of trouble in my life. Most of it never happened."

FRUSTRATION AND RELATED EMOTIONAL STATES

Frustrations and emotional states such as irritations, annoyances, stress, aggression, threat, and conflict often overlap. In this section, we will examine these relationships.

Frustrations, Irritations, and Annoyances   We get annoyed when something noxious recurs or somebody repeats a behavior we find offensive. This behavior also frustrates us because it impedes our wish for freedom from annoyance.

We also see irritations as provoking. We feel frustrated and impatient or angry toward such motivators—some driver blocking

11

the intersection when you want to drive through, or a coworker who needles you about your appearance—you might feel annoyed by this person's behavior and also feel irritated, impatient, and angry. If it continues you might perceive the whole work atmosphere as exasperating.

Sometimes recurrent stresses and tensions build up to a boiling point, and we observe a paroxysm (a sudden violent outburst of emotion) directed at the source of annoyance, irritation, and frustration.

While annoyances and irritations involve frustration, you can feel frustrated and not annoyed or irritated. For example, in learning to play a video game, the invaders from space knock out your home base and you play the game again, only to lose to the computer a second time. Charged up with new strategy, you confront the invaders for a third time and this time hold your own. Although you might feel frustrated while you learn to play the game, you don't feel annoyed or irritated.

Stress and Frustration According to biological scientist Hans Selye, stress—a generic term for mental tension—refers to the consequences of any demand made upon the body.

When you feel stressed, the sympathetic branch of your nervous system gains dominance. Your system releases glucose from the liver and adrenaline from the adrenal gland into the blood stream to prepare you for a burst of effort. In this process, your respiration increases, hairs stand on end, and chemicals that allow blood to clot more rapidly flow into your blood stream. If your system repeatedly charges up in this fashion, eventually this reaction may cause physical damage such as ulcers or coronary heart disease, or pain in the form of stress headaches. Selye points out that certain emotional states like frustration "are particularly likely to turn stress into distress." Clearly, process frustrations will increase a person's risk of what Selye refers to as the irreversible physical damage caused by the consequences of continuing stress. Such stress he sees as resulting from "distresses" caused by frustrations stemming from a lack of purpose, boredom, unpleasant activities, and dissatisfactions with life—especially from a sense of lack of accomplishment. Indeed, research with both adults and children suggests that people who often feel frustrated and distressed, on the average, live shorter lives and experience more physical ailments than those who learn to master frustrations and stresses. So aside from improving the quality of your life, effectively managing life's stresses and frustrations may extend your life. In addition, if you can view frustration and stress as growth signals challenging you to join the high adventure of self-discovery, your body will probably respond positively by maintaining plasma-free fatty acid and systolic and diastolic blood pressure levels associated with reduced stress and risk for coronary heart disease.

Your ability to manage frustrations and eliminate distress also improves, according to physician Nedra Belloc, when you practice good health principles. Belloc, who conducted research on the relationship between the health practices and mortality of a group of about 7,000 men and women over the age of 45 found that those men who prepared their bodies to withstand stress lived an average of eleven years longer. Women who prepared their bodies to withstand stress lived an average of seven years longer. The health practices seem sensible and possible to implement. They include

1. Nonsmoking
2. Weight control
3. Moderate drinking (about one drink per day)
4. Adequate sleep (8 hours for men and 7 for women)
5. Regular breakfast
6. No in-between-meal snacks
7. Physical fitness activity, such as jogging, working out, or swimming (20 or more minutes every other day)

These good health practices in combination with body relaxation methods (stretch exercises, muscle relaxation, yoga, meditation, listening to pleasant music, warm baths, singing, pleasurable images, biofeedback, and so forth) helps prepare you to achieve a state of relaxed alertness and works as an inoculation against frustration's harmful effects.

Frustration and Aggression   Up until the early 1960s, psychology researchers and clinicians actively studied the relationship between frustration and aggression. The prevailing view during that period that frustration led to aggression had many supporters.

Other researchers saw the frustration–aggression model as both too sweeping and too simple. Leonard Berkowitz, for example, proposed that we need to focus on other considerations to understand the relationship between frustration and aggression. These include

1. Motives the aggressor ascribes toward others
2. The person's attitude toward the problem area
3. Past learning
4. The person's interpretation of his emotional reaction to the frustration conditions

Frustrations: Threat and Conflict   Threat and conflict overlap with frustration. In threat conditions, something challenges the individual's integrity or basic drives. In conflict, the person faces opposing forces. Whichever way he moves, he risks unwanted consequences. For example, a person who dislikes her mate but fears living alone has a conflict she will have trouble resolving. Thus, she will frustrate herself whatever she does.

Psychological theorist Kurt Lewin described several conflict conditions. These include conflicts between two desirable alternatives (a young woman can marry only one of the two men she feels attracted to); conflicts between two undesirable alternatives (an impatient employee waits in line to pick up theater tickets for his employer; he hates to wait in line, but also cringes at the thought of his employer's reaction if he fails to get the tickets); and conflicts between simultaneously desirable and undesirable alternatives (a hypoglycemic person wants a piece of strawberry cheesecake but will feel depressed, sweaty, and anxious after eating the cake; she wants to avoid the symptoms but wants to eat the cake). Thus, conflict has the potential for producing frustration because each conflict situation contains both an obstacle and a choice.

FRUSTRATION TOLERANCE TRAINING

Aesop told a frustration tale that became a classic. A boy stuck his hand in a jar of filberts and filled his hand with the nuts. When he tried to withdraw his hand it got stuck in the neck of the glass. He did not want to let go of the filberts, but he could not withdraw his hand while he held onto the nuts, so he burst into tears of frustration. Like the boy with the filberts, when we attempt too much at once or refuse to face reality, our tolerance gets tested and we often fail the test. In contrast, frustration tolerance blends with mental flexibility and acts as a swiveling base that allows us to turn, move, and grow in many directions. When we think flexibly, we take half as many filberts and get both our hand and the filberts out of the jar.

While we may categorize frustration-tension (a feeling) as neither positive nor negative, how we create and respond to the tension may prove beneficial or dysfunctional. For example, an optimal and realistic frustration or tension can motivate positive action. On the other hand, a vague negative attitude can cause tension, promote intolerance, and lead to dysfunctional behavior such as confusion.

If frustration tolerance seems so pivotal to mastering challenges and coping effectively, then we need to define frustration tolerance to better understand it. I define frustration tolerance as the capacity to manage frustration, delay gratification (when required), and face problems. It can involve a decision to delay actions that can momentarily increase tension. For example, a dieting person who develops a craving for sweets but avoids eating a chocolate bar temporarily lives with the tension of not satisfying that craving. The investor who feels tense about the ambiguity of the stock market does research and watches trends until he has the data to make a knowledgeable decision about investing.

We can train ourselves to tolerate and master our frustrations. *Frustration tolerance training* derives from a common-sense observation: We have greater tolerance for frustration when we think of ourselves as effective and efficient in facing and resolving frustration problems. In effect, *frustration tolerance training* involves learning to clearly define our frustrations, setting a course to manage or master them, then following that course.

Stoically tolerating frustration has limited value, however, unless coupled with learning ways to *master* our frustrations. While we will probably never bat 1,000 in our encounters with frustrating conditions, we can learn to get the upper hand over most of them by learning and practicing frustration management skills.

We can live with a certain degree of unresolved frustrations, ambiguities, and inconveniences in our lives, so we don't have to face and resolve every frustration we experience. However, we should learn to recognize and deal with the relevant ones. For as all sailors know when confronting high waves, heading into the waves provides greater safety than allowing the waves to get astern. To head into the waves of life we can use a frustration tolerance training process that involves

1. Recognition of the frustration
2. Analysis of the frustration
3. Development of frustration management skills
4. Application of frustration management concepts
5. Utilization of feedback to improve coping skills

In this process we learn an awareness of the scope of our frustration problems; the implications of our actions; personal competencies that we can use to deal with the frustration; the coordination between how we think, feel, and behave; self-inquiry; delaying gratification; and adding fresh ideas to our frustration management skills. We will consider these seven points throughout the book.

YOUR NEXT STEP
IN CONQUERING FRUSTRATIONS

In the next chapter we will look into low frustration tolerance. We will also explore what the psychologist George Ainslie terms specious reward—going for the short-term counterfeit solution to our frustrating problems. We will discuss this human tendency to go for the easy (not necessarily best) solution when we consider low frustration tolerance and discomfort dodging.

People often give in to impulse because they don't want to tolerate discomfort. *To deal effectively with our frustrations, however, requires that we develop a certain tolerance for them.* Our low frustration tolerance can thwart our efforts at the outset unless we develop an awareness of it and learn to manage it.

LOW FRUSTRATION TOLERANCE

Two hours after Bernard Green awoke that morning he wished he had stayed in bed. Several things had gone wrong. First, he couldn't get his key out of the door as he tried to lock his apartment. Next, he got into a traffic jam and crept along the highway at a frustratingly slow pace. Arriving at work one hour late, he found a note from his employer, Mac Ryan, that read: "See me immediately." Worried that he might get fired for his lateness, he rushed to see Mac. He felt panicked as he prepared to defend himself. Alas, Mac had left the office to go on a trip. Now Bernard would have to wait several days before he found out what Mac wanted. However, the more he thought about Mac's note, the more he worried, the more urgently he wanted an answer, and the faster his troubled thoughts flowed. At this point Bernard shouted to himself: "Damn, nothing is going right! I can't stand it. I feel like quitting. Mac is a lame brain—he doesn't care if a person has a good reason for being late. Why do these things always have to happen to me . . . it's unfair."

Although we could hardly blame Bernard for feeling frustrated, we also can see that he blows things up in his head. For example, he made up the things about his boss not understanding, about getting fired, and so forth. Furthermore, we know nothing about Mac's intent when he wrote the note—he may have had to leave unexpectedly and wanted to let Bernard know. Aside from his trou-

17

bled fantasies, Bernard told us about his perception of those events when he said "I can't stand it." He told us that he really couldn't stand the inconveniences, hassles, and accompanying feelings of frustration tension and would pay any price to rid himself of distress. This willingness of desperate men and women to pay any price to override the frustrating ravages of the mind probably inspired Goethe to write *Faust*.

In Goethe's *Faust*, Mephistopheles (the devil) convinced Faust, an aging doctor of philosophy, that he could become young again and have Gretchen, the maiden of his dreams. To obtain this, Faust had to serve him after death. Faust, on the brink of suicide, agreed. Faust got what he wanted for a little while, but as the poem ends, the devil gets his due and drags Faust down to the underworld, condemned to spend eternity in hell.

Goethe's poem echoes a classic message: the expedient way often proves hardest.

People who feel impatient and can't tolerate inconvenience often overreact when they feel a strong urge to throw off the feeling of frustration. This strong urge to vanquish frustration, without much forethought, we call low frustration tolerance—a sometimes debilitating condition that practically always interlocks with emotional distress.

In this chapter and the next we will examine low frustration tolerance—its causes, forms, and solutions. By learning to recognize and manage low frustration tolerance, you can do much to minimize its destructive effects.

WHO HAS LOW FRUSTRATION TOLERANCE?

We exhibit low frustration tolerance when we avoid our problems instead of facing them. For example, when we party to avoid necessary work or cheat on a diet, we exhibit low frustration tolerance (LFT). This LFT problem takes on many disguises. It occurs when we refuse to discipline ourselves so that we can reach an important goal. It occurs when we think we can't tolerate inconvenience and use escape routes to avoid hassle. It shows up when we exhibit poor listening skills, finish other people's sentences for them, and keep ourselves distracted. It surfaces when we constantly want things to come quickly and easily. Consequently, even though an under-standable human response, low frustration tolerance often leads to poor results.

The following cases illustrate LFT.

Sally hates waiting. She always wants to hurry the process, so she impatiently turns the oven up to broil and unwittingly produces a dry unappetizing casserole for herself and her guests. However, the casserole incident only scratches the surface. Sally often feels rushed and impatient when getting ready for work, writing reports, reading the newspaper, waiting for a phone call, and so forth. She feels so rushed and impatient that she generally finds it hard to concentrate on most activities. Sally's behavior illustrates one form of low frustration tolerance.

Sandy has a weight problem. She fasts to lose weight, then nibbles and overeats when she feels frustrated. She wants to lose forty pounds and maintain a svelte 118-pound curvacious figure, but she continuously thwarts her intent. Consequently, she frequently feels flustered, frustrated, and angry, and eats to avoid thinking about her sorry emotional and physical state.

Vic acts like a menace on the highway. Whenever another driver blocks his path, Vic will blink his lights and ride the other motorist's bumper. If the other driver does not respond according to Vic's demands, he will pull sharply in front of him. He thinks that will teach "the creep" not to mess with him. Fortunately, Vic has yet to get into an accident. On occasion, however, some aggressive drivers take offense and retaliate by veering in front of him. Vic invariably feels shook-up during such combat and feels relief when it ceases, but still repeats this foolish pattern.

Luther can't tolerate sloppiness. If his wife or children fail to keep things in place, he gets furious, shouts, and calls them names. Inevitably he feels baffled when he meets staunch resistance. "After all," he thinks, "I ask only for a reasonably clean and neat home." While Luther feels quite justified in his demands, his family reports: "He's driving us crazy with his pickiness." Indeed, his son can't wait to grow up so he can leave the house, and his wife feels driven to have affairs in order to feel a sense of worth. Luther's wife's compulsion to have outside affairs also proves irrational when viewed under the psychological microscope. Why should a person have to have an affair to feel worthy?

Luther feels so compelled to keep things in order that a minute scarcely passes that he does not complain and blame. While we might agree that maintaining an orderly environment has advantages, we might also agree that the intense, urgent manner in which Luther seeks to maintain order fosters added interpersonal problems and symbolizes an emotional disturbance.

Bif, a physician, rarely arrives on time for work or for his appointments. His chronic lateness results from poor time management: he waits until the last possible minute to dress and gather his materials and consistently underestimates the time it takes to deal with details. Even though many of his patients have adjusted to his lateness, the long delays have resulted in a shrinking practice. His lateness in arriving for his hospital tour has become a joke among his colleagues. They comment that his patients get well and walk out on their own before he arrives. Despite the embarrassing consequences arising from his chronic lateness, Bif remains oblivious to the solution to the problem, but not to the frustration it creates.

Sally, Sandy, Vic, Luther, and Bif exhibit different forms of low frustration tolerance. Underlying the different symptoms, however, we find common threads. For example, each hates hassling himself and feels rushed, impatient, and frequently dodges frustration even at the cost of repeating unwanted patterns. Our low frustration tolerance gang has much in common with the Type *A* personality syndrome group.

THE TYPE *A* PERSONALITY AND LOW FRUSTRATION TOLERANCE

The Type *A* personality, whom Meyer Friedman and Ray Rosenman described in their popular best-seller *Type A Behavior and Your Heart* illustrates the principle of low frustration tolerance.

According to Friedman and Rosenman's report the Type *A* person operates "under the gun." He or she feels driven by a strong sense of urgency to accomplish objectives and often chases about trying to get things done. Strained by impatience, this individual risks a coronary. Thus, the pressured and busy manner in which he approaches life's challenges can ultimately prove not merely self-defeating but fatal.

Research on modifying the Type A coronary-prone behavior pattern conducted by Jeffrey Levenkron, Jerome Cohen, Hiltrad Mueller, and E. B. Fisher suggests that anger and impatience "are useful treatment targets and that change in them may not require more generalized personality modification." Anger grows from low frustration tolerance and gains propulsion from concepts such as self-righteousness and demandingness that fuel dysfunctional impulses to punish others who stand in one's way. Even when the angry person triumphs through punishing others, he loses because his chronic anger and impatience put him at risk for coronary heart disease.

Type A personalities can change by developing a philosophy based upon concepts of tolerance and correction rather than intolerance and condemnation. This book describes many approaches in which to accomplish this critical switch.

LOW FRUSTRATION TOLERANCE, A BIDIRECTIONAL PROCESS?

In some cases, low frustration tolerance promotes organized and productive action. For example, some Type A individuals operate efficiently in their work because of actions directed to avoid frustrations. Low frustration tolerance could act as a helpful signal that impels us into productive action. For example, the individual might get charged up to act then settle into an organized and purposeful response pattern. Generally, however, low frustration tolerance results in decreased efficiency, especially if it leads to disturbed thinking and impulsive, overly restrictive, or self-defeating actions.

LOW FRUSTRATION TOLERANCE AND DISCOMFORT DODGING

Low frustration tolerance coupled with disturbing thoughts about those uncomfortable feelings can lead to *discomfort dodging—*

escaping frustration tensions or seeking to avoid circumstances that might elicit frustration.

Not uncommonly, those who routinely try to dodge their frustrations and tensions limit their experiences and restrict their potential to handle problems effectively.

WHAT FUELS LOW FRUSTRATION TOLERANCE?

Some of us come into this world with a short fuse or a natural LFT tendency. Albert Ellis, psychologist and founder of The New York Institute for Rational Emotive Psychotherapy, has suggested that we may well have an inborn tendency to develop an LFT reaction pattern. According to Ellis, "virtually all human beings have a strong biological tendency to defeat themselves by being short term hedonists and going for immediate and not long term gains."

If we have strong intolerance for tension, we may have more to feel frustrated about because fewer things seem right or perfect. We activate this tendency when we magnify our frustrations, sometimes to the point of feeling psychologically disorganized.

HOW WE LEARN TO AVOID FRUSTRATIONS

Somewhere along the line, some of us get the impression that we need to avoid frustration and embrace comfort. We get help in this from many sources: advertising, the educational system, parents, and especially ourselves.

Advertising specialists have glorified products that pretend to ease frustrations and discomfort, such as pills to take away minor tension and stresses. The advertisements for those "tension reducing" products imply that people should not have to tolerate discomfort and can take pills to alleviate the tension. This same propaganda finds expression in advertisements for people who want quick and easy weight loss. People persist in buying these products in spite of questionable proof of their effectiveness and clear evidence of their negative and sometimes dangerous side effects.

The educational system often inadvertently fosters frustration avoidance. Procrastinating students make up excuses for failing to turn work in on time and sometimes have those excuses accepted. Some learn that they can occasionally get away without working, so they try to duck assignments. Parents contribute to their children's discomfort-dodging skills when they allow them to avoid reasonable frustrations simply because the children say "I don't want to" or "I don't feel like doing it now."

You can readily see that occasional successes in avoiding effort increases the likelihood that such avoidance efforts will continue. Fortunately, occasional successes in *mastering* frustrating circumstances also increase the probability that those behaviors will continue. The type of effort that dominates—avoidance or confrontation—depends upon the person's perception of where the reward lies for any given action.

While we can fix blame on many outside influences, people who avoid frustrations contribute to their own low frustration tolerance. The more effort we put into avoidance, the more likely we will create the self-fulfilling prophecy that we cannot handle tension.

FRUSTRATED EXPECTATIONS AND FRUSTRATION DISTURBANCES

When "comfort" expectations get frustrated, as they inevitably will, LFT people may try to evade hassles by adopting a perfectionistic outlook. They establish unrealistically high standards and, of course, fail to meet them. Such standards evolve partially through training and partially through the hope that perfection will compensate for imperfection and will result in the elimination of discomfort.

The idea of perfection compensating for imperfection to avoid discomfort seems perfectly absurd. How can a fallible and imperfect human ever expect to achieve the level that his natural imperfections prevent him from achieving in the first place? For example, too many conditions exist over which one simply has no control: daily variations in ability, unanticipated changes in the environment— all contribute to unpredictability in daily living.

This mental parody of avoiding discomfort through perfection contains a message—the person fears she will break down and collapse unless completely in control of the situation. Indeed, any person who fears intense feelings such as frustration or fear could disturb himself by panicking at the *thought* of experiencing strong negative emotions. And thus, the need for control contributes to a loss of control.

THE FRUSTRATION DISTURBANCE PROCESS

People who expect to have complete control over themselves and their environment and/or who fear tension will inevitably feel frustrated. The following describes and defines this frustration-disturbance process.

1. We perceive that we can't have what we want when we want it and feel frustrated, or our expectations fail to materialize, or our assumptions don't match reality.
2. We tell ourselves that we can't stand getting thwarted, and this form of self-talk starts the frustration-intolerance process rolling.
3. We repeat this message and become fixed to the idea that we should not experience frustration discomfort.
4. We preoccupy ourselves with thoughts of how onerous frustration feels and limit our chances to consider alternatives.
5. We overreact by withdrawal, aggression, rigidity, or impulsivity.
6. We rarely learn from the experience, because the high level of emotional interference disrupts short-term memory, and so we later repeat the pattern.

The process can happen quickly when we interpret potential frustrations in terms of LFT-evoking mental symbols or code words. For example, a person who first reacts to an impediment by exclaiming "Oh no!" may almost immediately feel a surge of tension shooting through his body that he becomes sensitized to, magnifies, intensifies, and tries to escape from. This process catapults him into a frustration disturbance—confusion, misery, a sense of loss of control, and so forth.

The frustration-disturbance process can also start slowly, as we frustrate ourselves by dumping more and more frustration-avoidance ideas into our emotional stew.

24

Most "normal" individuals periodically suffer from low frustration tolerance, as you will realize by reading this book. However, many people suffering from serious psychological disorders often suffer from chronic and intense low frustration tolerance. In reviewing the *Diagnostic and Statistical Manual* (DSM-III)—the "bible" for psychiatric diagnosis—I found that most of the functional disorders and many of the organic disorders have low frustration tolerance implied (but not stated or spelled out) in their symptom descriptions.

So you can see that we would be wise to consider frustration management a serious business and an important goal if we want to avoid disturbance and develop our competencies.

LFT LANGUAGE STYLES

Perception, thought, and language serve powerful directive functions. As neurophysiologist A. R. Luria has noted: "We have seen that speech enters integrally into the structure of mental processes and that it is a powerful means of regulating human behavior." In other words, a person who tells herself that she cannot endure something she doesn't like *and believes it* will intensify her frustration.

Specific self-expressions seem to relate to low frustration tolerance and/or frustration disturbances. These expressions include expletives to express exasperation, avoidance phrases (I don't want to, I can't do it), extrapunitive phrases (except for me, everybody and everything starts trouble), distress phrases (I feel overwhelmed), intolerance phrases (I can't stand it), imperatives (things should, ought, must, have to work out as I wish), self-reference phrases (I hate myself, I have no value), and helplessness phrases (I can't do anything right, I feel trapped).

By defining circumstances in terms of demands and distress, the frustration-disturbed person maintains a warped sense of reality. Unfortunately, the erroneous and overgeneralized language he uses perpetuates low frustration tolerance.

LOW FRUSTRATION TOLERANCE
AND SELF-CONCEPT

People with low frustration tolerance tend to perform below their capabilities and negatively distort their self-view. Such sophistry includes ideas that one has no value because of weak performances. The combined force of these self-defeating ideas and discomfort-avoiding tendencies causes these individuals to *act* incompetently, reinforcing their negative self-view and producing a self-fulfilling prophecy. The vicious circle of self-downing followed by problem avoidance leads to more self-doubts and feelings of inadequacy. People trapped in this pattern often involve themselves in a mountain of distractions, presumably to maintain a sense of comfort and security. Caught in this web, they fail to use their minds constructively to overcome false ideals and change painful patterns.

LOW FRUSTRATION TOLERANCE AND PROBLEM HABITS

The philosopher Socrates said, "all our faults arise from confusion and ignorance." While he exaggerated the issue, he seemed on the right track. If we can learn to identify and defuse the impact of our LFT language and false beliefs, we will spend less time confusing ourselves and have more time to develop our competencies and build quality into our lives.

Sometimes in attempting to abort the impact of our LFT distresses we develop self-defeating habits that temporarily divert attention from our LFT problem. Thoughtlessly following our LFT habit urges gratifies our wish to alleviate tension, and thus reinforces the habit. As we will see, however, LFT habits ultimately backfire.

The following five cases describe LFT habits and show the varied forms in which they appear. Following the descriptions, I outline a nine-point LFT-habit-breaking program.

June's problem habit, obsessive ruminations, causes her to feel emotionally upset. She wants to stop thinking about her troubles but can't. Kathy wants to lose weight but can't stay away from cakes and ice cream. Carl wants to quit smoking but keeps reaching for a cigarette. Will has a serious drinking and gambling problem. At the first sign of tension, he heads for the bar, then on to the racetrack. Selma feels an enormous urge to wash her hands. She fears going far from home—"What if I have an urge to wash my hands?" She gives in to the urge to wash her hands about thirty times a day.

Though their symptoms differ, June, Kathy, Carl, Will, and Selma all have compulsive problems. These problem habits seem to grow from *seemingly* irresistible urges that demand immediate gratification.

Most problem habits, including compulsive nail-biting, hair-pulling, or gum-chewing stem from a natural tendency to acquire habits in combination with stress and the erroneous belief that one *must* engage in the activity to get rid of tension.

You have many ways to break a low frustration tolerance habit. The following describes a nine-step habit-breaking approach:

1. Educate yourself about your problem habit.
2. Face facts and avoid excuses.
3. Try to look beyond the habit symptom to the problem.
4. Set reasonable and achievable goals.
5. Use your imagination to visualize the steps to your goal.
6. Make the habit a hassle by first doing something onerous before engaging in the problem habit.
7. Substitute something constructive for the habit.
8. Don't expect fast results.
9. Get help when you've tried hard and can't make progress.

You can break unwanted problem habits on your own. Despite the pessimistic statistics about the high failure rate of people who try to break habits through therapy and the high failure rate of those who join special groups, such as weight reduction and smoking cessation groups, millions of people *on their own* break problem habits. Those who don't often fail to work to develop effective frustration management skills or fail to execute the skills they possess.

In an influential article in the *American Psychologist*, Stanley Schachter reported new research on presumably difficult-to-control addictions. Based upon his research, he concluded that the prevailing professional and public beliefs that obesity, nicotine addiction, and heroin addiction "are almost hopelessly difficult conditions to correct is flatly wrong." He found that millions of people can and do clear themselves of destructive habits for long time periods, permanently in many cases. But to succeed, one must *intend* to succeed and *work* to break the habit.

THE ADVANTAGES OF OVERCOMING FRUSTRATION DISTURBANCES

Practically everyone suffers from frustration-related distresses and disturbances at various times, thus making them very normal problems. Conceivably, most of us could live with normal LFT problems as well as we could coexist with a hornet's nest in our back yard. But ridding ourselves of the hornet's nest reduces the number of painful stings we might receive. Analogous to getting rid of a hornet's nest, developing frustration tolerance and reducing frustration disturbances should provide us with some of the following advantages:

1. We more directly attain our goals.
2. We experience less emotional distress.
3. We tend to develop more constructive habits.
4. We experience greater emotional freedom.
5. We eliminate artificial barriers hindering our advancement.
6. We decrease internal stress.
7. We keep more focused upon our priorities.
8. We improve the quality of our judgment.
9. We improve our interpersonal relationships.
10. We remain more task-focused.
11. Our mental processes get clearer.
12. We shrink our destructive habits, such as overuse of medications, drugs, alcohol; smoking; compulsive sex; compulsive buying; pickiness; and overeating.
13. We improve the quality of our communications.
14. We upgrade the quality of our chosen life work.
15. We develop a wider range of personal, emotional, and action options.

LFT AND LAZINESS

Low frustration tolerance often gets confused with laziness. When I think of laziness, I think of a person who lacks ambition and has little interest in exerting himself. In contrast, I view low frustration tolerance as an active state, because the LFT-primed person expends considerable effort avoiding tensions. The lazy person has an apathy toward activity; the LFT person has an aversion toward discomfort.

People often use laziness as an excuse for withholding action. In most cases, "lazy" individuals actually suffer from LFT and lock themselves into this pattern by disclaiming responsibility. So, in this book, I will assume that most people who describe themselves as lazy actually use laziness as an excuse.

WHAT WE NEED TO KNOW TO MASTER LOW FRUSTRATION TOLERANCE

One of the main difficulties we have in mastering low frustration tolerance involves recognizing the process, as it does not always surface in the same way. For example, sometimes we react intolerantly to small matters, such as forgetting to buy toothpaste, and with great thought and tolerance to major life issues, such as divorce, death, and so forth. Sometimes we skirt major issues to avoid tension and obsessively ruminate over moderately important matters and inflate their importance beyond reason.

Low frustration tolerance also has the quality of an enigma. Sometimes the process follows a recognizable and predictable course. At other times the classic symptoms do not appear or don't appear in an expected pattern.

Frustration tolerance and low frustration tolerance do not constitute an all or none dichotomy. On some tasks, a normally high frustration tolerant individual may show a loss of efficiency due to low tolerance with that particular type of situation. Sometimes a person who tends to give up easily shows great tenacity under conditions others would have long abandoned. Therefore, if we can act tolerantly under some frustration conditions, we can learn to use this ability to change conditions where low frustration tolerance and discomfort-dodging dominate.

SUMMARY

Low frustration tolerance impels both productive as well as self-defeating actions. It probably links to our genetic predispositions, but gains direction from our perceptual and thinking processes. Although people who feel intolerant toward certain frustrating conditions may take appropriate steps to resolve these conditions, more often low frustration tolerance leads to poorly considered actions and to discomfort-dodging behaviors. Lastly, LFT can serve as the emotional catapult to frustration disturbances characterized by emotional oversensitivity and negative thinking.

Our ability to master frustration depends upon our ability to channel our frustration-motivated actions. If we bring our tolerance for frustration to a high level, this will help us to maintain a healthy perspective, an objective outlook, and a problem-solving focus. In contrast, low frustration tolerance may impede this process, because the person with a low threshold for frustration easily can spoil the results of her own efforts through nonreflective and expedient actions.

In Chapter 3 I will present a frustration tolerance inventory that will give you an opportunity to measure your frustration tolerance, isolate potential problem areas, and learn strategies for expanding your positive qualities.

CHAPTER THREE

TEST YOUR FRUSTRATION TOLERANCE

The physician and psychologist Herbert Birch told the story of a scientist who viewed the New Jersey swamp frog as an exceptionally stupid creature. The scientist observed that the frog would strike out his tongue hundreds of times at an impaled fly vibrating on the end of a pin surrounded by a cluster of pins. Each time the frog lashed out it cut its tongue and failed to eat the fly. So the scientist described the frog as an impossible learner—why else would it cause itself continuing pain?

Fortunately, other scientists noted that when the frog whipped its tongue out at a hairy caterpillar, it didn't strike a second time. Evidently it didn't like the taste and quickly learned its lesson. Because of this observation, this group of scientists concluded that the "intelligent" New Jersey swamp frog learned its lesson quickly.

While we may not resolve the question of the frog's intelligence, we might answer the question of why the frog struck at the impaled fly but not the hairy caterpillar. It seems that the frog doesn't associate sight with touch but does associate touch with taste. Consequently, the frog could not integrate information from what he saw and felt but could integrate the sensory data of what he saw and tasted.

Luckily, people can make connections between intrasensory information. They can integrate this information and come to conclusions. They can also make connections between what they see, what they think, and past experiences. But sometimes, like the New Jersey swamp frog, they have blind spots and fail to make critical connections. For example, people who think it unfair not to have their own way will apply this principle to virtually any situation in which they feel blocked. As a consequence, they self-inflict emotional pain just as the New Jersey swamp frog inflicted physical pain on itself.

At least part of this psychological blindness results from habituation to a self-defeating way of perceiving, thinking, feeling, and behaving. Part of this self-defeating process involves getting too involved in various distractions to the point that when your thoughts get tangled up with the distractions, you find it hard to concentrate on priority matters. Failure to *recognize* those distractors limits abilities and thus helps keep you caught in a revolving door of frustrations. I designed the following inventory to put a spotlight on some of these psychological blind spots.

THE LOW FRUSTRATION TOLERANCE INVENTORY

The low frustration tolerance inventory contains examples of common ways LFT can surface. The inventory allows you to isolate and roughly measure LFT behaviors. Following the inventory, I'll discuss each item, what your response means, and provide self-help strategies.

Instructions   Read the inventory and make a written statement on a separate sheet of paper that confirms or disconfirms each of the eighteen inventory items. Then rate each item according to its frequency, using the appropriate category under *Frequency*: O = Often; S = Sometimes; R = Rarely.

Specifying what we consider often, sometimes, or rarely has problems from a scientific view. After all, people measure these dimensions in different ways. As a rough guideline, if you agree that an inventory item characterizes a segment of your behavior and that behavior happens daily, your response might fall into the category of sometimes or often. You can also make that determination on a relative basis. After you have written your response to the questions, make a "relative comparison"—pair each item against every other and classify the four items that occur with the greatest frequency as "often" and the four with the lowest frequency as "rarely." The rest fall into the category of "somewhat." Of course, a rare event may cause greater problems than a frequent one, so you also will have to take the intensity of your reaction into account.

The majority of the inventory items describe negative patterns. Consequently, the inventory may prove uncomfortable to review and complete *if* you record only negatives. So describe positive thoughts and actions as well as negative thoughts and actions, so that you have a balanced and objective picture of your inventoried strengths and weaknesses.

I did not construct this inventory as I would a standardized test. This means you can't use it to compare your response against a norm (the average responses of other people to the same inventory) and find out where you stand relative to others. Instead, I designed it as a frustration awareness task for low frustration tolerance patterns.

	FREQUENCY		
	O	S	R
1. I feel patient when I have to wait.	—	—	—
2. When I feel an urge to do something, I cannot stop myself.	—	—	—
3. I feel too controlled and restrained.	—	—	—
4. I feel hurried and rushed.	—	—	—
5. I calmly deal with frustrating circumstances.	—	—	—
6. If I can't solve a problem right away, I tend to give up.	—	—	—
7. I attend to my responsibilities quickly, efficiently, and on schedule.	—	—	—
8. I feel caught in a rut.	—	—	—
9. I worry about what people think of me.	—	—	—
10. I feel depressed.	—	—	—
11. I get bored easily.	—	—	—
12. People who act unfairly deserve punishment.	—	—	—
13. I feel plagued by my poor habits.	—	—	—
14. I listen attentively.	—	—	—
15. I speak clearly and to the point.	—	—	—

16. I feel afraid to assert myself.   — — —
17. I act stubbornly.   — — —
18. I sulk, pout, or complain when I don't get my way.   — — —

INVENTORY DISCUSSION

Some very unusual individuals may check all the positive categories on this inventory and actually act the part they describe. However, I've met very few of these individuals. Most of us fallible humans will find we have a number of undesirable thinking, feeling, and behaving patterns to change.

In the following section I will comment on each of the eighteen inventory questions.

1. I feel patient when I have to wait.
If you checked "rarely" on this item, you probably concentrate upon the inconvenience of waiting. However, you can *change the pattern.* For example, instead of stewing while waiting in line, use the time for planning a trip, developing an idea, or amusing yourself by watching the antics of impatient people.

2. When I feel an urge to do something, I cannot stop myself.
If you checked "rarely," you probably see yourself as thoughtful, reflective, and purposeful. If you checked "often," you've categorized your actions as impulsive. An impulsive individual acts without much forethought in order to avoid an uncomfortable situation.

Impulsiveness and spontaneity often get confused. "Impulsive" refers to poor self-control. It comes from a feeling of emotional stress. Spontaneous behavior, on the other hand, voluntarily arises without inner restraint and appears natural but directed: you hug someone you like.

Impulsiveness, like impatience, declines when reflective thought intervenes between the impulsive urge and the compulsive action that normally follows. "Thinking it out" allows for a wider range of alternatives and a higher level of response. Thinking it out helps *liberate the mind* from impulsive thoughts.

Albert Ellis's rational emotive therapy system provides a simple *A-B-C* frustration management approach you can use to short-circuit impulsive thinking. In the *A-B-C* system, *A* stands for the activating event, *B* for the belief about the event, and *C* for the emotional consequence. To defuse impulsive thinking, you pause when you first feel an impulsive urge, then articulate what you believe about the activating event, and finally you examine the validity of your belief. For example, if you think you can't tolerate delay, ask yourself what makes delay so intolerable? By asking probing questions geared to examining the validity of the beliefs underlying your urgency, you can put the situation into perspective and then consider alternative ways for dealing with it. In this way you avoid getting yourself tangled in the *A*'s and *C*'s by demanding that the *A*'s change in order for the *C*'s to change when the real problem lies with the *B*'s.

3. I feel too controlled and restrained.
The inhibited person suffers from "analysis paralysis." He stifles his own spontaneousness by thinking too much. Not uncommonly, this self-doubting individual appears uptight and feels uptight. Paradoxically, the restraints the person imposes to inhibit discomfort inhibit the person and promote discomfort. The inhibited person finds it difficult to let go. However, prudent risk-taking sometimes helps. For example, try some new experiences, such as experimenting with different styles of behaving.

Experience has shown that people who involve themselves in carefully planned behavior assignments can establish functional new behavior patterns. For example, one of my clients felt inhibited about wearing a bathing suit on a public beach because she didn't have a perfect figure. She feared that people would stare and criticize her. To overcome this inhibition, she went to a remote beach early in the season. After she felt comfortable sunning herself with few people present, she went to more crowded beaches as the season advanced. Through this progressive desensitization technique, she was able to sit comfortably on a crowded beach and not worry about what people thought about her.

4. I feel hurried and rushed.
If you checked "often," you probably need to develop your planning and organizing skills. Rushing and falling behind schedule occur either when you bite off more than you can chew or will accept nothing less than complete and perfect work.

You can feel rushed for other reasons. Perhaps you have a problem saying no because you fear rejection or conflict. Sometimes rushing occurs when you think you have oversold yourself and think you have to live up to your reputation and deliver your best work at maximum speed. Perhaps you ignore reality—although you can make deadlines under perfect conditions, such conditions rarely happen outside the realm of fantasy.

Good scheduling requires a realistic balance between what needs to get done and the time available to do it. Prioritizing the work, segmenting the top priority, and assigning time to do each segment often helps you work "smarter," not harder, and to function at a relaxed and productive pace.

5. I calmly deal with frustrating circumstances.
If you checked "rarely," you may tend to overreact. That spells trouble, because when you overreact, you direct your attention inwardly and may miss some vital outside clues.

Overreactions can occur in different forms: rumor, minutia, and diversionary.

The "rumor" form starts when the person tells himself that something unpleasant might happen, then feels and acts as though it had.

The "minutia" form starts when the person makes too much out of too little. For example, you fail to get the morning newspaper on time and make several nasty calls to the newspaper and kick the family dog.

The "diversionary" form occurs when the person carries on about an uncontrollable problem and evades the controllable ones. For example, when a person bemoans worldwide corruption instead of preparing for an upcoming examination.

Overreactions, like a spreading virus, need containment through developing a realistic perspective. By placing an event in perspective, we can see it as one part of the mosaic of life.

6. If I can't solve a problem right away, I tend to give up.
An "often" response suggests that you need to develop goal persistence. People who give up easily follow a recognizable pattern: They tend to get easily distracted, often have a poor sense of timing and pacing, and commonly exhibit a strong desire to dodge discomforts.

People get themselves into this bind when they misinform themselves about the concepts of easy and simple. For example, the idea of backpacking across the United States sounds simple enough; however, the action of the plan may not prove easy.

While no *easy* solution exists to extinguish this problem, a *simple* solution does! Breaking the back of this dysfunctional pattern begins with honestly facing the facts that some things in life will feel uncomfortable and will take time to change.

7. I attend to my responsibilities
quickly, efficiently, and on schedule.
If you responded "rarely" to this question, you may frequently put things off or procrastinate because of poor time management, a poor self-concept, and/or discomfort dodging. If you have an extreme case of putting things off, you may feel overloaded by many demands and responsibilites.

To master that disturbing feeling it helps to back off and pick a place to begin. Then invest the time and energy to take the first step in the process of clearing up the work. Breaking the project down to do-able bits and working on each bit helps get a new counterprocrastination pattern started. (Knaus, W., "Overcoming procrastination," *Rational Living*, 1973, 8, 2–7). In Chapter 9 we will take an in-depth look at procrastination—its causes, forms, and solutions.

8. I feel caught in a rut.
An "often" response suggests that you find yourself in a rut, tied to a mundane, energy-sapping, unproductive routine. This group includes the middle-aged housewife who mindlessly watches soap operas, the person stuck in a dead-end career, and the person who doesn't allow time for leisure activities.

Low frustration tolerance, depression, and fear coupled with self-doubts serve as barriers to *changing the rut pattern*. A person in a rut has a major challenge to make a healthy lifestyle change. Fortunately, some ruts yield to activity remedies that involve altering parts of your daily routine by selectively introducing novelty and challenge into your life. For example, take a different route to work, try out a new hobby, plan a vacation to a place you've never visited before, or just make one small change in your routine each day.

9. I worry about what people think of me.

If you checked "often" or "sometimes," you may want to tune in to your own self-talk about what you really fear. Do you, for example, think you only can have worth and comfort if certain people respect you?

When a person fears disapproval, he experiences a psychological fear, because he interprets disapproval as a threat to his self-esteem.

The person who constantly worries about rejection acts like a mind reader who thinks he knows people's thoughts and feelings. Mind reading can get you into trouble. For example, if a person assumes that his new coworkers don't like him, he might act resentfully and his coworkers might find his behavior unappealing and avoid him for that reason. Thus, he would fulfill his own prophecy through attributing feelings to his fellow workers that they probably did not harbor originally.

People who worry about what other people think of them often place too much value on obtaining people's goodwill. Consequently, real and imagined social shuns become magnified out of proportion.

When the cover of psychological fear gets pulled aside, we find that the person with status worries actually suffers from an intolerance for tension. He believes he must shelter himself from experiencing discomfort and has a case of symptom discomfort— a fear of the feeling of social discomfort.

10. I feel depressed.

If you checked "often," you probably pessimistically dwell on the negatives in your life and psychologically depress yourself.

Psychological depression consists of a grouping of demoralizing mental concepts—hopelessness, helplessness, a sense of ineptitude, and low frustration tolerance. Dealing with such self-defeating elements takes time. No easy solution exists. However, like any psychological problem, insight into the process, refusal to perpetuate it, directly challenging depressing ideas, developing positive thinking habits, and willing oneself to engage in counter-depression actions often provide the conditions for change (for a more detailed map for overcoming psychological depression, see *How to Get Out of a Rut*, Knaus, 1982).

11. I get bored easily.
Boredom generally reflects restrictive thinking. Chronically bored people take the passive position of waiting for someone to entertain them or something to stir them out of complacency.

A certain amount of boredom creeps into anyone's life: we must do some mundane activities; periods of relative inactivity normally occur; interludes do exist between exciting activities. However, if weariness, tedium, and boredom routinely invade your life, try to anticipate pleasurable experiences, plan for those experiences, and enact your plan.

12. People who act unfairly deserve punishment.
If you checked "rarely," you probably view yourself as a highly tolerant individual who can accept wide variation in human behavior. Of course, this response may indicate that you have too much tolerance for unacceptable and/or irresponsible behavior and wonder why you or others get blamed for having acted irresponsibly. If you checked "often," you probably could profit from exploring how to make fewer condemnatory value judgments and learning how to develop a more tolerant outlook.

When we judgmentally damn others for failing to act according to our script, we fail to recognize that some attitudes and behaviors we consider unacceptable legitimately cause no harm to anyone. In other words, if the action doesn't cause you or anyone else harm, why condemn it?

13. I feel plagued by my poor habits.
If you checked "often" to this question, you might determine what negative purpose the habit serves and consider positive alternatives for overcoming it.

Some habits, such as compulsive gum chewing, smoking, picking at your skin, hair-pulling, and so forth, serve as tension reducers. Typically, they intensify during periods of stress and subside when the stress abates. Often they get so well-practiced they have a "life of their own" and persist only because they have become pervasive habits.

We may develop habits that make life easy in the short term but soon inconvenience us. For example, the person who leaves clothing hanging about everywhere or fails to take the time to organize his tools or work adds hassles to his life.

Certain negative habits seem difficult to break because the accompanying urge or compulsion seems very strong. However, as you act against negative habits, you give yourself an opportunity to build tolerance for tension as well as ridding yourself of the habit.

14. I listen attentively.

In this culture, communication skills—including listening skills—carry high value. Yet, most of us could substantially improve in this area.

People who hear but don't listen generally don't attend carefully to what others say. Sometimes they get caught up in mental monologues that distract them from hearing what others say and hear only fragments of the conversation.

Many people listen with an inattentive ear. Colin Cherry's classic experiment on the "cocktail party syndrome" illustrates this point. Cherry's experiment demonstrated that cocktail party conversations seem punctuated by sequential digressions—each person waits for a break in the conversation to shift attention to his topic.

You can improve your listening skills when you concentrate upon understanding the speaker. This process involves learning to recognize and eliminate egotistical talk, aimless digressions, and defensive chatter, and replacing it with attentive listening.

15. I speak clearly and to the point.

Effective speaking skills, especially public-speaking skills, have much value. Good speaking skills, like good listening skills, require concentration and practice to develop. However, since many people would rather die than get up in front of an audience, this often requires a radical change in attitude. Change requires action. Action

40

requires making an effort. So effort has to comprise part of any action. And effort produces stress.

Raymond Cattell, a well-known personality theorist, described "effort stress" as an effort made in the service of forcefully grappling with reality. He implies that a person who puts more work into solving real problems and experiences more effort stress will also likely experience less fear. So learning to overcome public-speaking tensions requires making an effort to overcome those inhibitions.

Practicing the speech and getting feedback from a friend, taking a speech class, trying to express an idea comfortably within five to ten seconds, or speaking without distracting pause statements, such as you know, uh, uhm, and so forth, help improve speaking skills and build public speaking confidence.

16. I feel afraid to assert myself.

People who don't assert their self-interests often suffer confrontation anxieties, and/or feel they don't deserve what they want. To expunge this LFT pattern start with learning how to articulate and express your interests and wishes, finding a common ground in disputes, and recognizing that interpersonal communications include listening, sharing, requesting, persuading, and insisting.

17. I act stubbornly.

A stick-to-your-guns reaction makes you appear uncomfortable with compromise, perhaps because you believe you will lose status if you give in. Worse, yet, you fear you might come under someone else's control unless you defend yourself.

Stubbornness results in frustration and other forms of tension for those involved. Fortunately, this process can yield to a task-focused outlook if the person comes to view the quality of interpersonal communications as holding greater value than victory in a contest of wit.

18. I sulk, pout, or complain when I don't get my way.

Sulkers, pouters, and complainers duck problems. While not bad people, they do present themselves as unpleasant characters.

Like most low frustration tolerance reactions, sulking and pouting represent acts of expediency. Such people often fail to directly express their wants and feelings. When these individuals learn to speak up directly and effectively, sulking and pouting diminish.

Complainers prefer to grieve over problems rather than to solve them. They often act both superior and helpless, and thus present themselves as knowledgeable victims. George, for example, thinks his supervisor, Eleanor, hasn't a brain in her head. He thinks he could do her job better than she. His brooding actions make him appear inept, and he periodically gets chewed out for his poor performances. But rather than work to do a superior job and get recognition (and possibly a promotion), George lapses into complaining and views himself as a victim of the system.

Complainers need to look into the question of what they expect complaints to accomplish that positively directed actions cannot.

In the following section we will look at change strategies, problem solving, and values clarification as methods for *liberating the mind* and *changing the pattern*. These processes add to our understanding of how to manage our low frustration tolerance urges and show us how to move toward greater emotional freedom.

PART II

BASIC PROBLEM-SOLVING APPROACHES

Many fraudulent solutions exist to solve the problem of how to master frustrations. One such solution involves joining a cult and letting someone else do your thinking for you. As an alternative, you could try to get "blissed out" by buying time at a joy enhancement resort where you spend time chanting, taking steam baths perfumed by natural swamp water, meditating, and listening to the local guru pontificate. These and other "make me better" solutions usually offer a false hope that can cause you to put time into benefitting someone else's enterprise as you become less reliant upon yourself to solve your own frustration problems. As the ancient philosopher Epictetus said, "Whoever would be free, let him wish nothing which depends on others, else he must necessarily be a slave."

Those who want to change for the better often find it difficult to break undesirable patterns. This difficulty often proves frustrating, but if we want to develop our competencies, we have to make the effort to effect change. In this effort problem awareness, problem solving know-how, and concentrated efforts will serve our purposes better than using hit-and-miss tactics to reduce our frustrations. Also, we probably will not overcome our frustrations rationally by putting our lives in the hands of some "guru."

In Part II, we will look into what we have to do when *we* do the work to conquer our frustrations. We will examine the process of change, how to employ effective problem-solving strategies, and the role values have in the development and resolution of problems and frustrations.

Chapter 4 describes a pathway to follow to liberate ourselves from self-constricting barriers and to actualize our potential. Chapter 5 describes how to solve frustrating problems using time-tested approaches. In Chapter 6 we look into the relationship between our values and our frustrations. We will try to separate our true values from false, vague, uncertain, or imposed values.

CHAPTER FOUR

THE PROCESS
OF CHANGE

Jody, one of my 12-year-old clients, blamed her father for all her discontents. "He never lets me do anything fun," she moaned, with tears of anger welling up in her eyes. Then she went on a further indictment of him. When I jokingly said, "Perhaps we ought to stand the guy up against the wall and have a firing squad blast away at him for the heinous crimes he's committed against sweet innocent you," Jody interrupted to say that maybe she contributed to the problem.

The child contributed to her own problem with her father because of her LFT self-talk and narrow perception of fairness. In effect, she had become so enmeshed in complaints that she failed to accept her share of the responsibility for the squabbling. She also failed to recognize that things we want normally don't come popping out of a magician's hat at the flick of a golden wand. But once she begrudgingly acknowledged that she contributed to the conflicts, she could alter her behavior and reduce her frustrations.

Jody quickly realized that she had choices other than getting angry. And since getting angry didn't seem to help her get what she wanted, she decided to find out what alternative ways of behaving would work best for her. Also, since she definitely did not like the sensations of anger, she decided to see if she could *liberate her thinking* by *changing her pattern*. For example, she wanted a puppy. Her dad had refused, claiming that he didn't think she would take care of the pet, and the burden would fall on him and her mother. So she read a few books on how to select and care for a dog, spent a few days talking to dog owners and veterinarians, then spoke to her father about the dog he had as a boy. When she stopped blaming her dad and started communicating, she found she could convince him to get her a dog. More importantly, she learned an alternative way to resolve her frustrations and saw that the changes she made led to *growth*. Thus, personal growth results when we experience healthier patterns.

Like Jody, we sometimes habituate to self-defeating inter-actions. Once habituated, we often fail to envision our role in the creation of our frustrations and instead project the blame onto others. This defensiveness gives us a poor perspective on reality, and thus we continue to frustrate ourselves and inhibit our ability to adapt.

In this chapter we will cover a variety of topics addressing the process of change. The topics include 1. the inevitability of change, 2. the five stages of change, 3. self-perception theory and com-petency, 4. the importance of self-correction, 5. if you want some-thing, do something, 6. the concept of helpful restrictions, 7. talk your way through it, 8. preparation counts, 9. practice.

THE INEVITABILITY OF CHANGE

Two stress-management psychologists, Thomas Holms and Richard Rahe, published an article, frequently quoted, that lists a number of potentially positive as well as negative changes that we could experience. These include the death of a mate, marriage, the birth of a child, career shifts, winning a lottery, and so forth. Both positive and negative changes represent stress events. The researchers gave a numerical weighting to each event and found that if a person experienced over 300 units of stress within the period of a year (the death of a mate would measure about 100 units, a change in community activities might measure about 10 units, and so forth), then the person's accident proneness or health risk would elevate. For example, 80 percent of people with high life-stress units got sick or involved in an accident in the following year, compared with 20 percent of the low life-stress group with 150 or fewer stress units. However, despite the ominous prediction that an accumulation of multiple major and minor changes can result in illness and accident, the person with sufficient coping resources can learn to deal with each one separately and not let them accumulate. Thus, though difficult at times, he or she can put such events into perspective.

Grappling with significant life events makes change part of the process of growth and maturity. However, times exist where we may not see this. Too often in times of great sadness or mounting frustrations we find it tempting to give in to our frustrations and build barriers that can lock us into a frustrating and self-defeating lifestyle.

We sometimes have to pry away self-defeating barriers by putting ourselves through a growth process that involves recognizing how we create our own frustrations and altering our habituated and limiting patterns.

Sometimes change and growth come slowly, and we go through stages in this process. In this chapter I will consider a five-stage process of change and describe concepts you can apply to work through the stages.

THE FIVE STAGES OF CHANGE

A number of years ago my colleague Ed Garcia (a psychotherapist) and I collaborated on a theory that we believed depicted the process people go through when they make positive changes. We viewed such positive changes as catalysts for growth.

Let's begin by looking at the difference between change and growth. For example, if you broke a leg, you'd quickly recognize the change. Few, however, would define such a change as growth. We'd see it as an alteration. Growth, on the other hand, we'd see as increasing or expanding our positive capabilities. The positive growth change theory goes as follows.

We all complicate our lives in myriad ways. Most complications prove unnecessary and restricting, as when we create needless frustrations because of our own contradictory motives. For example, some people make comfort a priority: they don't want to do anything that will cause them to feel uncomfortable or deprived. These same individuals also may want to control their lives and improve their skills. But improvement involves change, and change can often feel uncomfortable. So the choice becomes that of choosing between comfort and change. Under such conditions, choosing one priority clearly frustrates the other.

This concept of contradictory motives only scratches the surface. We create other complications when we demand perfection of ourselves, approval from others, and complete control over the events of our lives. These impossible goals create unnecessary frustrations that draw us away from dealing with our real problems and frustrations. We move toward the development of our positive capabilities as we free ourselves from thoughts that pollute our minds and instead fill our minds with healthy, logical, creative, and imaginative thoughts.

We grow and develop our best qualities and capabilities through what we call the *five stages of emergence:* awareness, experimentation, integration, acceptance, and actualization.

1. *Awareness* serves as the first stage of emergence. The journey to self-understanding and frustration mastery begins when we become aware of what we want, how we trick and divert ourselves from achieving it, and what we can do to change.
2. *Experimentation* serves as the second stage of emergence. By seeking new experiences and learning by experimentation, we come to broaden our outlook and develop new skills and awareness.
3. *Integration* serves as the third stage of emergence. As we begin to experiment with our reality-testing abilities, we begin to see more clearly the relationship between our self-concept, feelings, and actions. In this stage we have a "feeling understanding" of the meaning of change generated from our own concrete experiences. We experience a feeling understanding when we go through an experience, process what we experience, and understand how we feel and why.
4. *Acceptance* serves as the fourth stage of emergence. We accept ourselves, others, and reality because we understand the truth of what we see.
5. *Actualization* serves as the final stage of emergence. In this stage we feel active and propel ourselves into relevant experiences with a fresh eye.

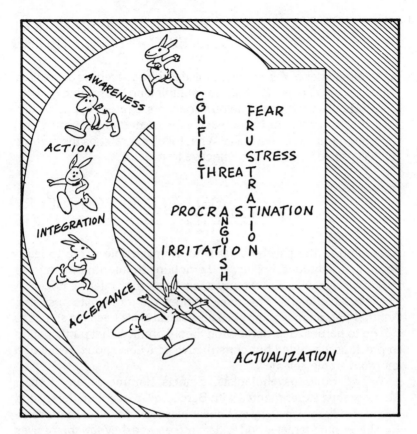

This theory represents Knaus's and Garcia's observations of the stages people evolve through their journey to self-realization. In this process we can suggest new awareness by questions, actions, or statements; we can encourage constructive experiences and experiments; and as therapists we can provide feedback in the form of guidance, interpretations, and reactions. However, in the final analysis the individual creates his own awareness and must internalize, integrate, and accept what he experiences. Thus, the theory represents an awareness-and-action approach to change: integration, acceptance, and actualization can only grow from awareness and action—and can only occur within the individual's own psychology.

AWARENESS ACTION
CONCEPTS AND STRATEGIES

In the remainder of this chapter I will describe awareness and action concepts you can use to organize your thinking to promote growth.

Virtually hundreds of helpful concepts, strategies, and tactics exist that can aid you to increase your frustration tolerance and frustration management skills. What follows scratches the surface but will provide you with an effective framework.

SELF-PERCEPTION THEORY
AND COMPETENT SELF-PERCEPTIONS

According to the psychologist D. J. Bem, people come to learn about their attitudes, beliefs, and emotions by inferring them from their own behavior. For example, a person may infer he does not possess athletic ability because he does not participate in sports. Another person may think she lacks social skills because she does not go to parties. Self-perception theory predicts that participating in previously avoided but constructive activities should result in a more favorable self-view.

Two other psychologists, Francis Hammerlie and Robert Montgomery, experimented with Bem's self-perception theory and found that heterosexually anxious males learned to act more comfortably around females and to date more when they saw themselves as competent in relating to women. The increased sense of competency came about as a result of their own actions.

But what happens if you try to act competently and don't succeed? The following section addresses a significant concept, the "necessity of failure."

FAILURE AND THE IMPORTANCE
OF SELF-CORRECTION

Let's begin with an example of this process. A young man flunked out of medical school then spent his time around Cambridge, England, exploring rocks and beetles. His father declared him a failure.

Yet Charles Darwin shed the prophecy of failure by continuing his studies and work, even though others doubted him. He went on to write *On the Origin of Species*—a major contribution to the field of biology. While Darwin's theory of evolution had precedent (Aristotle noted the ordering between worms and man long before him), his work ushered in a new era in the study of biology.

Failure ranks with death and taxes as one of those inevitabilities of life. As an inevitability *and* as a potent source for frustration, we'd better learn to deal effectively with this experience.

When one fails, she falls short of the standard against which she evaluates her performance. Consequently, we view failure as definitional. We could, for example, define failure out of existence by defining attempts to meet a standard as "test runs" or experiments. Under experimental conditions we use the results of the experiment to guide our future actions—including developing new experiments.

Instead of defining failure out of existence, let's accept the term and not fear the concept. For example, sometimes the results of failure have negative implications. At other times they have positive implications, as the failure points to the pathway of opportunity. However, many people fail to take reasonable non-life-threatening risks due to their fear of failure. In this section we will consider reasonable risks that people sometimes fear to undertake. But first let's look at the concept of risk-taking.

Sensible risks, such as spending extra time trying to develop a new account if you work as a salesperson, may not produce quick positive results. But the risk provides opportunities to do better than we might have done otherwise. Yet many people avoid such risks. Why? Although no universally acceptable answer exists a common one does. Risk-aversive people blend the concept of caution with risk because they define risks as *dangerous*. After all, when in danger one would wisely move cautiously.

Thus, overly cautious individuals often miss opportunities. People who fail to take risks and don't get anywhere often feel frustrated by a lack of progress. Frustration can lead to hostility which can prove a greater threat than risk-taking, because the frustrated and hostile person will tend to experience greater sensitivity to threat. He may preoccupy himself with negative thoughts of "danger," mobilize himself to meet the threat, and behave like a modern Don Quixote—fencing with the "windmills of his mind." In such an emotionally charged atmosphere vicious circles proliferate, such as looking at people with suspicion, watching them pull back, then getting more suspicious of their motives for retreating. This risk-aversive mental trap melts when we start to think of risks as presenting opportunities. It also diminishes when we start to rationally measure the costs of the venture over the potential benefits and stop thinking of danger and failure.

While practically everyone periodically feels uncomfortable about the prospect of failure, some of us have a dread of what failure implies. At least part of the dread grows from the conviction that one's total human worth links up to each inadequate action. This peculiar idea grows from inflexible and lofty perfectionistic expectations to which we adhere. And the person who thinks this way habitually measures himself against what he lacks. When a person thinks his human worth ties to isolated performances and the performance standards seem so lofty they "fly with the eagles," we can readily understand why the person fears failure.

Some people go to extremes to avoid failure. Work-a-holism characterized by persisting and pressuring oneself to the point of fatigue constitutes one extreme. Choosing to work at an occupation in which one finds herself overqualified constitutes another. Excuse-making to cover up ineptitude constitutes a third. A fourth includes getting involved in an enterprise with no personal investment, because failing then constitutes little cause for concern. For example, a gourmet cook opens a pizza restaurant because he worries that his more exotic work might not receive rave reviews.

Some people dodge opportunity in order to avoid possible failure because they fear what it *feels* like to fail. Such discomfort-dodging behaviors generally reflect a threat to the person's self-esteem. Fear of failure, then, involves both a threat to self-esteem (a form of frustration) and intolerance for that form of frustration.

Failure-sensitive people elevate their expectations and standards beyond reason. Interestingly, most seem above average in their intellectual ability; some exhibit superior intellectual abilities. But they use their intellect in the service of trying to live according to ideals rather than in facing the sometimes difficult and concrete realities of life.

People who fear failure, who adhere to high standards, and who claim to value human worth and dignity often have trouble answering the value question: If you value human worth and dignity, then how do you justify adhering to standards so strict that they exclude you from experiencing worth and dignity?

In contrast to those who fear failure, people who effectively manage their problems and frustrations typically examine the cause(s) for their failures and proceed to correct them.

You simply cannot make progress without some experiences that fall short of what you desire. Indeed, this concept of the necessity of failure corresponds with the famous Swiss developmental psychologist Jean Piaget's well-tested theory that humans learn through assimilating new information and comparing it against existing knowledge structures. If the old structures don't match, the person accommodates to the new learning. This mental system works remarkably well unless the person blocks his own awareness by mentally distorting uncomfortable new ideas.

The person who sees reality clearly will have a number of distinct advantages. The more varied a person's experiences, the more varied his ways of looking at his problems. The more tolerant of frustration, the more likely that he will accept failure as part of the learning experience. The more a person keeps open to his experiences, the less likely that he will fall into the trap of viewing life through a psychoscope: a narrow, stereotypic, rarely changing outlook. The more tolerant person with a sense of perspective will also "fail" to fall victim to viewing life through a kaleidoscope of bewildering patterns of changing values and scenes.

To learn and to grow rich in experience and clearheadedness means taking reasonable risks that include failure as a possible outcome. The importance of this concept resounds in inventor Thomas Edison's reputed response to the question of how he felt after 50,000 failed attempts and summarizes the spirit of the concept of failure acceptance: "At least I now know fifty thousand ways in which it won't work."

IF YOU WANT SOMETHING, DO SOMETHING

We can manage low frustration tolerance through applying tested psychological strategies. This section outlines the *if you want something, you have to do something* strategy. A brief case presentation of a five-year-old child illustrates the application of this concept. The child, Karen, had a habit of throwing objects (especially groceries when she went shopping with her mother), breaking dishes, uprooting plants, and causing trouble.

As a result of her therapy, she soon concluded that if you want something, you have to do something. Knowledge of this pivotal concept helped her change her destructive pattern. Karen learned the "want something, do something" concept through a let's pretend game in which I asked her to teach me what she says and does when she goes to the grocery store.

After Karen explained how she knocked groceries from the shelf, I pretended to walk through a grocery store throwing items from the shelf. Next, I checked to make sure I had accurately acted out her part. The child agreed that I had. Then as I carried out the act, I gleefully remarked: "Oh, boy, what fun throwing the groceries. I can't wait to get spanked and sent to my room when I get home." After I mentioned the consequence, Karen shouted out that the spanking wasn't supposed to be part of the story. "But isn't it?" I asked. "After all, don't you get spanked? Doesn't your mother stop you from watching *The Muppet Show*? Don't you get sent to bed when you get home?" Karen got the point.

Although the want something, do something idea seems obvious, my young client did not see how she impeded herself until she experienced the obvious: if you want to cause problems for yourself, you have to work at it. And while we often think of "want something, do something" as promoting positive results, we can bring about results we do not want and then fail to see the cause.

Furthermore, the idea that if you want something, you have to do something has great importance in overcoming low frustration tolerance. Clearly, to manage low frustration tolerance and to act in your own interests involves restricting dysfunctional actions and promoting adaptive ones. In other words, if you want to experience the negative consequences of low frustration tolerance, such as tension, avoidance, and procrastination, you merely indulge the urge. If you don't like the outcome, you work to think and act so as to promote the results you desire.

THE CONCEPT OF HELPFUL RESTRICTIONS

Any potentially effective problem-solving process involves recognizing the problem, defining the goal, and planning what to do about it. It also requires that we develop an understanding of *how* we block ourselves from achieving our goals and *how* to get unblocked. It also includes the desire to change, getting involved in the process of change, and restrictions. You stick to activities that lead to your goal. For example, losing weight requires restricting excessive food intake and practicing that restriction.

This concept of restrictions proves helpful for people who want to lose weight, for five-year-old girls who want to maintain privileges, or for anyone who tires of repeating self-defeating behavior patterns.

Some people think that any form of restriction limits freedom. Paradoxically, certain restrictions allow for the *development* of skills, competencies, and emotional freedom. An alcoholic, for example, who restricts his liquid intake to only nonalcoholic drinks has greater freedom than the alcoholic who drinks whatever and whenever he wants. The free-drinking alcoholic has a lifestyle that centers on a very limited range of experiences.

The principle of restrictions applies especially well in accumulating capital. The person who refrains from impulse-buying has the hope of developing dollar resources for the future. Fewer than one person out of 100 knows both how to save and how to invest money wisely. Although most of us would like to conserve our funds, we find ourselves using too much of our income to purchase harmful products, such as cigarettes or junk foods, or paying too much interest on installment plans. People who want to save money must avoid costly self-indulgences and impulse purchases. These restrictions can result in greater financial freedom.

The principle of restrictions also applies to developing good interpersonal relationships. For example, one of my clients met a work-a-holic, taciturn surgeon whom she immediately envisioned as an ideal marriage partner. A major part of the fantasy involved what she considered his marvelous dedication to his profession and the prestige that his position carried in the community. Before her second date, she dwelled upon marrying this man and having six kids. Although daydreams need not cause harm, the intensity of her desires gained such momentum that she made herself anxious at the prospect of making a slight mistake in her dealings with this individual. Then she feared she would act uptight. She began to eat to get rid of her tension. Then she felt tense because she started to gain weight. Clearly, she had to restrain this unrealistic mental prattle so her thoughts and actions could flow spontaneously. She had to restrict her fearful thoughts by convincing herself that 1. She needed to gather information about this seemingly wonderful person before dedicating her life to a daydream; 2. Her selective perceptions grew from a "needing" framework (compared to a person who wants something but can live without it, the needing person irrationally believes she *has to* have what she wants or won't survive emotionally); 3. She would have to consider that she would spend her married life relating to the person, not to his profession.

TALK YOUR WAY THROUGH IT

Self-restrictions can lead to greater self-control. However well-meaning our wishes to benefit from restrictions, low frustration tolerance can snafu our best intentions. Part of giving in to urges to immediately self-gratify results from failing to verbalize clear instructions to ourselves. This exclusion can leave our project resting at the inception stage: We've thought of what we want to do but don't carry through our thinking and acting.

The clinical researchers Donald Meichenbaum and Joseph Goodman took an old truism, "talk your way through it," and conducted a series of experiments to determine whether verbalizing instructions to oneself can help guide positive actions and reduce impulsive actions. In their experiment they asked their subjects to first talk out loud to themselves and tell themselves how to solve a problem. Next, to whisper the same instructions. Third, to think the instructions. These researchers found that impulsive children and adults better solved their problems when they followed this pattern.

The system works as follows: Suppose you have a speech to deliver in front of your local Chamber of Commerce group. In the past you received the criticism that you talk too fast and don't pay enough attention to your audience. This time you intend to slow down and talk *to* your audience instead of talking *at* them. So you tell yourself out loud (preferably in private), "I will speak slowly and try to get my ideas across to the group." Then you whisper this same idea to yourself, then you think it.

A few simple rules help in using this system:

1. Keep the self-talk instructional.
2. Keep the instructions simple.
3. Keep the instructions brief.
4. Rehearse the instructions several times, including at least once just before tackling the problem.

Meichenbaum and Goodman's structured self-talk method applies to conditions where making self-guidance statements helps improve the action.

This instructional sequence of audible self-talk, whisper, and sub-vocal talk can cause a shift in focus from acting on impulse to acting with purpose. When this shift takes place, it may do so because you've practiced a new operating rule that reminds you to counter a dysfunctional habit and build a functional one.

As you might surmise, self-instructional talk has wide applications for dealing with potentially frustrating circumstances: preparing to deal with unpleasant people; preparing to break an undesirable habit such as gum chewing; preparing to solve a mathematical problem; and so forth.

So when you face problems you have approached previously with unsatisfactory results, try this instructional rehearsal process and talk your way through the steps to self-improvement.

PREPARATION COUNTS

People can develop psychological fears when they prepare inadequately. Instead of working they worry.

Positive instructional self-talk strategies can prove helpful in a program of self-guidance. However, self-instructions don't go far enough if they don't include behavior rehearsal. For example, a person may give herself wise instructions concerning how to deliver a speech but become tense and fearful due to inadequate preparation. Such inadequate preparation might include failing to develop and organize the content of the speech and failing to practice the delivery. Some fearful people do prepare, however, but do so with fear intense enough to disturb their ability to memorize and retrieve material.

Individual differences exist in people's abilities to develop public-speaking, musical, or social competencies. So we should not expect that preparation alone will make up for what we may lack in talent. However, many of us fail to discover our competencies because we don't consistently test them out.

Preparing adequately for many of life's responsibilities involves expending effort in thought and practice. Failing to take the time to prepare often leads to psychological fears and the tendency to rationalize for failing to act. Adequate preparation can help rid oneself of the need to make excuses, can reduce stress and frustration, and can impact positively on self-image, confidence, and competence.

To sharpen preparatory skills it helps to examine where the breakdown in the preparatory process occurs. Do you bog down at the decision stage—you can't determine what to do? Do your efforts get diverted shortly after you start the project? Do you stall yourself out in midstream? Do you nearly finish, then fail to put the necessary polish on the product you've worked hard to develop?

Each breakdown phase requires a slightly different interpretation. For example, if you bog down at the decision stage, what do you think you'll lose if you choose one direction over another? If you drag your heels at the inception stage, you may think the project will take too much time or you won't get up the speed to complete it. If you stall out in midstream, do you build up task-resistance because you overburden yourself with thoughts about the tiresome nature of the project, think about the fun of doing something different, and then divert yourself to that new project? If you fail to put the final details toward the project, you may believe that you don't deserve to succeed.

So if you find that preparation routinely proves one of your weak points, why not try to understand and change the reasons for why you stop yourself? Chapter 9, which describes how to overcome procrastination and stop frustrating yourself, expands upon this breakdown issue.

In contrast to people who don't adequately prepare, some people overprepare and mess up their performance. Fearing to appear unprepared, they set a very difficult, sometimes impossible, goal—having total knowledge or perfect skills. Such perfectionistic individuals get tied up in their own psychological shoelaces, overwhelm themselves with the enormity of the task, frighten themselves because they don't think they can finish on schedule, and build a resistance to future efforts because of the onerous way they have defined their present task. Not uncommonly, these overstructured, compulsively ordered, discomfort-dodging individuals don't enjoy themselves, because they get too fixated on following poorly conceived self-created rules.

PRACTICE

A famous learning theorist, Edward Thorndike, thought at one time that practice alone makes perfect. Later he modified this position to say that practice with knowledge of results leads to better performance. People who improve their performance use knowledge of results to correct their actions.

Thorndike's dictum reflects the spirit of the "necessity of failure" concept. Without failure, no need exists to take corrective actions. Reality teaches us that the person who dedicates himself to a purposeful and productive effort will periodically fall short of his standards, but he also shapes and refines his work through this process. The practice of revision constitutes a form of practice that often results in quality creations.

Although practice may not make for perfect work, practice with feedback can help develop skills. And the more skillful we get, the more likely we will come to enjoy what we do, and the more we will want to repeat it, thus providing us with more practice.

The person who begins to develop a new skill flounders at first, then picks up speed as his initial experiences provide a structure for new learning. The old pro, on the other hand, makes fewer discoveries because he has mastered the basics as well as the advanced material. But practice has something for the new learner as well as the old pro: the former rapidly gains skills; the second employs the skills he's developed and refines them.

In the following chapter, we will take a close look at problem solving as a way to add strategy and dimension to your efforts to master your frustrations.

CHAPTER FIVE

SOLVE YOUR FRUSTRATION PROBLEMS

Aesop tells the story of a hungry fox who tried to jump up to grab grapes from a vine. Alas, he had no luck. As he ran off, he stuck his nose in the air and exclaimed: "I thought those grapes were ripe, but I see now that they are quite sour."

WHAT CONSTITUTES A PROBLEM?

Like the fox and the grapes, people also have problems. For both foxes and people a problem exists when we have a disparity between what we want and what we have *and* that condition contains unknowns *and* requires evaluation and solution.

Some people, like Aesop's fox, feel frustrated when they don't know how to solve a problem—the "don't know how" constitutes the barrier blocking goal-directed behavior. We can also feel frustrated if we *do* know how to reach our objective but somehow can't. For example, a fearful person may know how to give a fine speech but fail to manage his public-speaking fears. His real problem involves learning to minimize or neutralize his public-speaking fears.

In contrast to Aesop's fox, those who accurately define problems, develop reasonable alternative solutions, and enact the most promising problem-solving strategies tend to have fewer disturbing frustrations and enjoy life more. Furthermore, they have little cause to mask their frustrations with "sour grapes" rationalizations and thus will get more "ripe grapes." Most important, they will know they have a powerful tool—problem-solving skills—to use in learning to master frustrating circumstances, build confidence, and develop frustration tolerance.

To begin our journey into the world of problem solving, let's look at the work of problem-solving expert Karl Duncker. According to Duncker, a problem arises when we have a goal but don't know how to reach it. He notes that whenever we can't get to where we want to go by action, we have the recourse of thinking how we might achieve our objectives. Duncker notes that problem solutions—at least to practical problems—must fulfill two requirements: they must result in attaining the goal and the results must come through action. In solving practical problems we may strive for the more elegant solutions but use expedient or interval solutions on the way.

PROBLEMS, CONDITIONS, AND FRUSTRATIONS

While problems and frustrating conditions seem similar, differences do exist. Whereas problems contain unknowns, frustrating conditions may not.

Frustration may result from a condition that requires acceptance or management. For example, aversive weather conditions may force a cancellation of your weekend plans. If you have no reasonable alternatives, you may simply have to accept the disappointment. You may have a serious coronary condition and can no longer play handball, your favorite sport. You may, however, decide upon an alternative activity like hiking that proves far less strenuous yet still provides exercise.

In addition, frustrations may arise from problems, but problems need not evoke perceptible levels of frustration: in some instances a problem evokes excitement, a state of determination, or a professionally detached response. However, when we feel frustrated, we feel tension, regardless of the level of importance or duration of the problem—no tension, no frustration.

In this chapter we will look at how to manage frustrating problems and conditions using the problem-solving process. To this end I will discuss fifteen problem-solving topics that include the myth as a vehicle for demonstrating the problem-solving process, the art of stating problems, and the eight problem-solving steps.

PROBLEM SOLVING: MYTHS AND HISTORY

What humanity has accomplished came as a result of identifying problems, finding solutions, discovering that those solutions created problems, and then finding ways to solve the new problems. By their nature, problems often generate frustrations. So our history overflows with examples of frustrating problems. As Columbia University mythology professor Joseph Campbell has noted in *The Hero of a Thousand Faces*, trials, tribulations, and frustrations invade the human condition. *How* we meet these challenges tells the tale of our lives. In this context, historian Arnold Toynbee's views about civilizations apply to the individual: many challenges exist; we will meet some; we will not meet others.

But we can learn much from mythology and history concerning the problem-solving process. In this section, we will consider the myth as a model for this process. Moreover, we will consider what history teaches concerning the *evolution* of problem-solving efforts, as we can gain much from our past in learning to master our frustrations.

In Homer's *The Odyssey*, the poet told of the Trojan War's aftermath and of how the Greeks celebrated their victory in drunken revelry. Caught in the swell of narcissistic glory on the night of their triumph, they failed to give tribute to the Olympian gods who had helped them to win. In anger, Athena, goddess of wisdom, and Poseidon, god of the sea, decided to destroy the Greek fleet. The gods created a fearful tempest that struck the fleet and sent Odysseus' ship careening far from its course and Odysseus himself into an adventure that spanned ten years.

In attempting to return to his native island, Ithaca, Odysseus faced numerous obstacles, problems, and challenges that he overcame. These included the Cave of Polyphemus, the Sirens, Scylla and Charybdis, Circe's witchcraft, and the Land of the Dead. All of these challenges required Odysseus to find problem solutions. Examples appear in stories, myths, and fairy tales that encapsulate the problem-solving process. While stories such as Homer's epic seem farfetched, they often present some truth about the problem-solving process for those with imagination to see beyond surface meanings and into the story's deepest structure. These stories describe the skill, wisdom, courage, dedication, and "can do" mentality that frequently prove vital to developing problem solutions.

EVOLUTION AND PROBLEM SOLVING

When we observe the results of problem-solving efforts throughout history, we see wheels, crop irrigation and rotation, the existence of spoken language, writing, books, immunization against deadly disease, canned goods, refrigeration, the automobile, the existence of large multinational corporations, a credit system, and so forth. At some time or other, someone recognized the existence of certain problems—such as how to preserve food—and did something to solve it. For example, let's suppose that one of our Cro-Magnon ancestors wanted to find a way to preserve food. Perhaps by design, he or she found that the family meat supply would last longer if placed in a watertight skin and stored at the bottom of a cold creek. In the generations that followed, others refined the solution or found new solutions—thus, we presently have canned goods, preservatives, and refrigeration growing from our original need to preserve food.

A review of history tells us that problem solving in one area alone can span centuries, such as evolutionary discoveries of how to preserve food. Our review also teaches us that insights and advances often build upon our earlier progress. Psychologist Edward G. Boring describes the culmination of ideas and the emergence of a new thought or breakthrough as the *Zeitgeist*.

At certain times in history, breakthrough ideas occur. Problems get solved when time, place, and need all stand ready for the change.

We see an example of the breakthrough in what Edward G. Boring wisely noted about American functional psychology: No person invented functional psychology—James, Dewey, Ladd, Baldwin, Cattell—nor gave it to America as a gift. It was there when it was there because the time and place required it.

Although the Zeitgeist normally refers to the ways we discover things about our world and how we solve environmental problems, the concept also refers to the evolution of self-knowledge. Through accident, planned experiments, observations, insights, and feedback, we gradually develop the awareness and action skills to identify and resolve "personal" problems when time and place require it.

Philosopher of science Thomas Kuhn has written that a long accumulation of knowledge may lay the foundation for new discoveries. However, according to Kuhn, sometimes a "paradigm shift" takes place. This occurs when a crisis arises requiring a traditional problem to undergo redefinition in order to find new solutions. So, according to Kuhn, problem solving can occur as a result of a long accumulation of study and work *or* when a revolutionary new idea comes on the scene that better solves the problem. The new communication technologies serve as good illustrations of a paradigm shift. We can apply Kuhn's paradigm shift concept to personal problem solving. For example, your mate threatens to divorce you because she claims you don't spend time with her and the children. You don't want a divorce so you radically shift your perceptions and decide to go out with her every Saturday night and plan an activity with her and the children every Sunday afternoon.

THE ROLE OF EXPERIENCE IN PROBLEM SOLVING

Another expert problem solver, physician, and experimental psychologist, Herbert Birch, presents considerable evidence to support the importance of experience in problem-solving. He found that people and animals that have had direct exposure to the various elements needed to solve problems tend to come up with insightful solutions. Those with limited or meager exposure find it difficult to see relationships, because they have a more limited frame of reference from which to draw inferences. For this reason we generally see the bookworm intellectual as an impractical person trapped in a world of ideals. He or she often has little practical experience to draw from and must rely upon secondhand experiences transferred through the written and spoken words of others.

Our knowledge grows from accumulated experiences. We can apply this knowledge to novel situations and perhaps add to it. We may also explore new fields and contribute new ideas that "experts," attached too much to the ideologies of their systems, do not see. Eric Hoffer's "true believer" describes experts who attach themselves to an ideology. Those who adhere to the ideology as though no other viable viewpoints exist operate out of a closed mental system.

As our experiences grow in variety and richness, we will feel increasing interest and desire to identify and resolve our problems, because we will have more flexibility to do so and will feel less pressured by burdensome thoughts of ignorance and inferiority.

DAILY PROBLEM-SOLVING OPPORTUNITIES

Our daily problems provide us with opportunities to confront barriers, overcome limitations, practice problem solving, and manage frustration. Problems offer us opportunities to sharpen our problem-solving skills. For example, if we want to risk capital by investing in oil field service companies, we must wisely assess the energy needs of the future and the value, role, and function of such companies. Inflation and high interest rates reduce our buying power, so we have to determine how to better control expenses. We can't find our lost pet and must think of where he might have gone. We can't understand the directions for filling out the state income tax form, so we seek a tax consultant or knowledgeable neighbor to help. We have a new job opportunity but don't favor the relocation area, so we must analyze the trade-offs. The kids have been inside for several days due to stormy weather, fighting and racing about. How do we redirect their energy?

Because so many different types of problems exist, it helps to classify them.

PROBLEM CLASSIFICATIONS

We have personal, public, self-interest, anticipated, emotional, and social problems. We have business, financial, political, scientific, and mathematical problems. We have practical, theoretical, and conceptual problems. We have resolved and unresolved problems. However, we can classify problems under four general headings: algorithmic, practical, emotional, and creative. The following describes each problem classification:

You solve *algorithmic problems* when you follow the right rules. Mathematical problems follow algometric procedures.

Practical problems arise when something happens and you *get pulled* into problem solving: your roof begins to leak on a rainy weekend evening; the landlord raises your rent twenty-five percent, and you think you already pay too much.

Sometimes practical problems get solved by trial and error, such as when you try random solutions in the hope that one will work. Practical problems often get resolved by reapplying what we learned in similar problem circumstances.

Emotional problems refer to self-created disturbances: you blame yourself for failing to think and act perfectly and thus fill yourself with feelings of worthlessness.

As with other types of problems, we occasionally might think that uncontrollable conditions cause our frustrations and emotional distress. For example, we manage a political candidate who gets arrested for drunken driving and assaults a police officer as the campaign nears its final days. Or our son or daughter falls in love with a person whose traits we view as undesirable. Or, we upset ourselves about mistakes from the past—we no longer have control over them, only over how we might reinterpret them. Perhaps we'd like to graduate with highest honors but have a learning disability that impedes our ability to concentrate. Or, even though uncoordinated, short, and female, we'd like to play on the boy's varsity basketball team.

Occasionally we view a problem as uncontrollable because we have convinced ourselves that we are victims of circumstances and we can do nothing. However, emotional disturbance only seems uncontrollable if the person classifies himself as incapable of managing his emotional affairs. This view can change. For example, some compulsive individuals view themselves as helpless to halt the compulsive act. However, once the primary problems get spotlighted and the person learns how to combat them, many seemingly uncontrollable problems, such as overeating or alcoholism, come under control.

People who frustrate themselves with self-created emotional problems often fail to see themselves as the masterminds of their frustrations. Instead, they often stand transfixed on their distressing feelings like a moth transfixed by a flame.

We get away from the "flame" and on to the solution when we apply a hardheaded scientific approach. We start by working to make an *objective observation* of the condition—a factual description of the condition we face. Next, we generate several explanatory hypotheses for our frustration. Third, we look for confirming or disconfirming evidence for each hypothesis. Last, we recheck the evidence and plan a course of action. In this process we may stop escalating the frustration and bring the causes into sharper focus. For example, we may discover that we disturb ourselves by what we tell ourselves. When we examine the language we use when we feel disturbed, we find that our thoughts overflow with low frustration tolerance language (see Chapter 2 for a review of this language system).

Creative problems occur when you go out of your way to seek experiences that might both frustrate and stimulate you to find a solution. You *pull yourself* into creative problems: you wonder if better ways exist to improve the work flow in your office; you wonder if you could discover a new theory to predict weather patterns. Creative problems intrigue inventors, philosophers, and all who seek to advance knowledge. Like the hidden figures in children's picture puzzles, such problems represent real challenges.

The psychologist Norman R. F. Maier describes creative problem solving as part of a process of productive thinking where we restructure and repattern past experiences to meet the requirements of the present situation. The physicist Norwood R. Hanson observes that inquiry can lead to *discovery* of new patterns and explanations outside the realm of reshuffling old concepts and "facts." Both Maier's and Hanson's views of productive thinking and creative problem solving relate to heuristics—an exploratory problem-solving technique that relies on self-educating methods, such as evaluation or feedback. I discuss this method in the following section.

HEURISTICS IN PROBLEM SOLVING

We often view creative problem solving as a heuristic process. Heuristics involve using rules of thumb for finding solutions to problems and include

1. Defining the problem.
2. Setting goals.
3. Finding analogies between the current problem and similar problems.
4. Considering or eliminating improbable solutions.
5. Varying or rearranging the elements of the problem.
6. Working backwards from a possible solution to the statement of the problem.
7. Clearing away all extraneous information.
8. Adding peripheral information.
9. Identifying the shortest possible route to the solution.
10. Specifying roundabout routes to the solution.

Heuristic methods do not guarantee success. Sometimes after you've taken preparatory steps you simply get stuck and frustrated without any bright ideas. When you get stuck, it often proves helpful to take a break from the problem, because it takes time for the mind to sort out the various possibilities and make new connections. A break allows you time to incubate solutions. Sometimes after a few hours, days, or months the solution suddenly appears like a blaze of insight. Unfortunately, sometimes you never obtain the solution you seek.

PROBLEM RECOGNITION: A PRIME CONSIDERATION

L. René Gaiennie of the University of South Florida School of Business Administration has noted that *problem identification* ranks as the most important step in the problem-solving process: "if you don't recognize the problem, you can't solve it!" Problem recognition requires an inquisitive mind, relevant experiences, and proper method. But problem recognition proves elusive if

1. We don't look critically at our present ways of solving problems.
2. We become complacent with our traditional ways of solving problems even if those ways prove weak or ineffective.
3. We develop psychological "sets" which predispose us to respond in predictable ways because we habitually see specific problem conditions in a preconceived manner.

Problem recognition can come from intuition, insight, mental connections, guidelines, or through guidance—education, reading, discussions, advice, and so forth. In each instance, properly framing the problem in question form helps clarify the problem.

STRUCTURING THE PROBLEM SITUATION

We need to get specific if we intend to problem-solve. A well-articulated question often sets the stage for that specificity. A well-defined problem allows us to decide the probable success of a proposed solution.

But articulating a question that provides direction for a solution may prove mercurial and frustrating—most people do not train themselves to specify questions that clarify problems and provide a structure for their problem-solving efforts.

The case of Wilfred suggests a structured approach for identifying and clarifying problems.

Wilfred's life had little direction. He felt adrift and frustrated— "I can't seem to get my act together." Although he held a responsible position as a travel agent, he found it difficult to throw himself into his work. He felt unhappy about his family life: He and his wife and two children seemed to lack a sense of unity. He had many talents but didn't get beyond thinking of how he might best use them. For example, he knew he did well training travel agents. Yet he took no substantive steps to exploit this skill, even though he thought he might like a career training travel agents.

Wilfred's first step out of his rut involved learning to discriminate between productive and nonproductive questions—if he couldn't ask helpful questions he couldn't expect to develop a clear statement of direction and purpose.

PRODUCTIVE AND NONPRODUCTIVE QUESTIONS

Questions can fall into productive and nonproductive categories. Productive questions provide direction and suggest ways of organizing thoughts and actions. Nonproductive questions appear ambiguous or ubiquitous. In this section I will discuss these two types of questions.

Returning to Wilfred's case, he originally asked the question: "What do I want to do with my life?" Many have raised this question; sometimes the question sets the stage for productive answers. But such ubiquitous questions rarely help define a beseiging problem. Indeed, ubiquitous questions often lead to an avalanche of vague, inwardly directed questions such as Why have I messed up my life? This closed question invites self-condemnation and inferiority feelings.

In contrast, productive questions frame problems in solvable terms. To generate such a question, Wilfred had to abandon vague questions. Instead, he needed to accurately define his problem.

THE SWLO METHOD

Wilfred's first step in this process involved gathering information that he could use to define his problem. To do so he would have to break from his convergent thinking pattern—trying to make new ideas and experiences fit with old fixated materials. Instead, he needed to adopt a divergent thinking style: thinking that reflects originality, creativity, and flexibility of thought. Thinking divergently allows us to look for problem solutions in uncommon ways. For example, if we make up answers then create questions, we think divergently. To cross over from convergent to divergent modes of thought, he used an SWLO method, whereby he specified his strengths, weaknesses, limitations, and opportunities.

Through the SWLO analysis, he identified and organized as follows: *Strengths*—good sense of humor, intelligence, interest in others, gregariousness, caring, honest, good analytic skills; *Weaknesses*—impatience, worrier, poor organizing skills, procrastinator;

Limitations—minimal savings, no advanced education, no supportive business contacts, family committed to the current neighborhood, economy in downturn; *Opportunities*—few qualified travel sales trainers, moderate turnover of travel sales personnel, available market for travel training program, large travel agency chains periodically hire trainers, job availabilities in private travel training schools.

Wilfred compared his self-assessment with his current lifestyle. From this comparison he framed the following question: What relationship exists between my drifting and poor organizing skills? The questions described a problem Wilfred could investigate and thus a direction he could take.

The SWLO format Wilfred used to help specify his problem provided an additional advantage: he could see strengths, such as intelligence and analytic ability, that he could apply to develop organizing skills. However, Wilfred's initial problem identification provided only a global direction—one that required further refinements.

GET SPECIFIC

Wilfred raised a question that hit at the heart of a major source of his frustrations: the relationship between his sense of lack of direction and his organizing skills. Scientific research often begins with such relationship questions. Most useful personal problem solving also starts with relationship questions: What relationship exists between my impatience and poor self-organizing skills? What conditions provoke worry? What do I tell myself when I cause myself to procrastinate? What relationship exists between my sense of lacking direction and impatience, worry, procrastination, and disorganization?

A good scientist does more than raise questions, she also specifies the meaning of the terms she uses. For example, what constitutes poor organizing skills in Wilfred's case? What does impatience mean, and how does the definition apply? This type of question serves a vital purpose in the problem-solving sequence, since such questions help pin the problem down, and thus help tighten the definition of the problem.

DETERMINE ALTERNATIVE ACTIONS

Once the problem gets pinned down, then a whole universe of problem-solving alternatives opens up. For example, once Wilfred decided he would work to develop his organizing skills, he had access to a large variety of viable action approaches. For example, defining his problem in terms of organizing-skills deficiencies made it possible for him to follow up by researching a large literature of theories, approaches, methods, and dynamics of organizing. This literature provided ample resources to draw ideas from to aid him in formulating his new organizing strategies.

Creativity theorist A. F. Osborn's brainstorming techniques can also help one to develop problem-solving alternatives. In traditional brainstorming, a task force has an assignment to solve a problem, such as how to improve machine utilization and efficiency at a candy packaging operation. During brainstorming, individual task force members say anything that comes to mind that relates to the problem. The wilder the idea, the better. Because we think associatively, one idea will trigger another. No idea gets criticized. Later, each idea undergoes evaluation, and we put the better ones into practice.

You can use a variation of the brainstorming process: Talk quickly and uninterruptedly into a tape recorder about one frustrating problem (you can also quickly write your associations on paper). As in regular brainstorming, you want to generate as many ideas as you can. In this phase, you don't make value judgments, evaluations, or criticisms.

Usually, about five minutes will suffice for this rapid-fire idea-generating method. During that five minutes, you can link your ideas together in an impressive number of alternative strategies to evaluate later. A few of your brainstorming ideas may supply exactly what you need. When Wilfred attempted this method, he generated a few good ideas he hadn't before considered, including researching the topic of how to get organized.

You can add to your brainstorming efforts by using a boundary disrupting trick that the Gestalt therapist Fritz Perls describes: Think of each idea you generate in terms of its opposite. For example, Wilfred generated in his original brainstorming session the idea "do nothing." The opposite idea, do something, led to an associated idea, do research.

Wilfred analyzed each of his brainstorming ideas. Once he decided which alternative(s) suited his purposes, he set his goal: to modify then apply the how-to-get-organized approach described in another publication (Knaus, 1979) to suit his special purposes.

SETTING GOALS AND PLANNING ACTION

Once Wilfred decided to improve his personal efficiency and effectiveness through the development and application of an effective organizing system, he started to plan the steps he needed to take. This planning included spelling out his objectives.

Goals and objectives differ. Goals define the end point against which you direct your efforts. Objectives represent the steps leading to the attainment of the goal. Each objective constitutes a minor end point that provides the platform for the next end point.

Once Wilfred established his plan of action, he organized his daily activities plan by creating a schedule of activities. This required him to establish the conditions for achieving his individual goals and objectives.

TAKING ACTION

So far we considered preparing for change by identifying, clarifying, and defining problems. We considered how to generate problem-solving hypotheses, analyze the options, create plans, and organize for action. Next comes implementing and controlling this change process.

Implementing and controlling refer to putting the plan into action and monitoring progress. This stage involves some risk: Your plan may prove inadequate; you commit much time to the undertaking; you expose your wishes and desires; you allow yourself to experience frustration; you have no guarantee that you will improve your conditions; and, you face the possibility that your situation will get worse despite your best efforts. However, when you consider the alternative of inaction, implementation and risk-taking may seem like the preferred direction.

THE EIGHT-POINT PLAN

The following eight-point plan summarizes the approach I've presented in this chapter. It overlaps with the time-tested scientific method. Consequently, you can look at your problem-solving efforts as experimental efforts. With experience, you will learn to refine this model and develop skill in solving frustration problems. If you want to test the system out, pick a problem from the inventories in chapters 1 or 3 or one of your own problems. Experiment using this eight-point structure and see if you can master that frustration.

THE EIGHT-POINT PLAN

1. State the problem in general form.
2. Complete a SWLO analysis of the problem.
3. Use a variation of brainstorming to generate alternative ideas.
4. Present the problem in the form of a question.
5. Specify the meaning of the terms in your question to assure that you have a clear definition of key elements of the problem.
6. Avoid diluting your efforts by trying to solve more than one problem at a time—stick to your one main problem issue before going on to the next.
7. Describe how you will organize your problem-solving efforts by prioritizing your alternatives.
8. Test your plan and use feedback as your guide to further change.

In Chapter 6 we will consider the relationship between values and frustrations and look into whether some of our frustrations rise from values conflicts.

CHAPTER SIX

FRUSTRATIONS AND VALUES

In the middle of the twentieth century, the eccentric economist Roger Ward Babson roamed the woods of Dog Town, a New England ghost town. Throughout those woodlands he chiseled inscriptions on rocks, imploring people to be on time, study, don't get in debt, and show integrity. He also chiseled sayings such as "when work ceases, values decay"; "never try, never win." Rather peculiar? Perhaps. However, whether they were peculiar or not, he left inscriptions of basic values that if followed can minimize many sources of frustration. For example, people who arrive on time, manage their finances, and test their skills by applying them in interesting new areas will probably have fewer problems to feel frustrated about.

Values can assert a relatively powerful organizing influence over our actions. These mental constructs give us our sense of good and bad, right and wrong, worthy and unworthy. They relate to matters we consider very important; thus they provide the genesis for our choices and decisions. For this reason alone, we would wisely know our values.

Unfortunately, many people grow to adulthood with no clear system of values. Others grow up parroting socially desirable values such as honesty or integrity without comprehending what such values involve. For example, incorruptible people have integrity. They don't take bribes, falsify documents, or distort the facts. Thus, people with integrity will normally hold to high standards. The person who parrots the value of integrity and yet only looks out for number one probably does not possess integrity.

While value systems operate as relatively enduring frames of reference, they can and do shift depending upon situational variables. We know, for example, that a normally truthful person will sometimes shade the truth. Generally, we can count on the person's truthfulness—his or her actions largely will reflect in truthful behavior.

We tend to behave consistent with our value structure. If we understand our *real* values—what we stand for—we have a better chance to live life with fewer frustrations, compared to the person with a confused value system who doesn't know where he stands from moment to moment. In the remainder of this chapter I will describe concepts and exercises that you can use to clarify your values as part of your program to develop mastery over frustrations. The topics include the acquisition of values, value choices, values and decision making, values conflicts, values and fraudulent goals, responsibility (a prime value), and self-help principles.

THE ACQUISITION OF VALUES

We develop our values in varied ways—trial and error, insight, reasoning, experimenting, imitation, accident, and so forth. We rarely learn values just because we hear other people preach the virtues of their values. For example, when professional moralists (priests, rabbis, ministers) preach values such as honesty, we may not incorporate the value based only on the authority's sermon.

Preached moral standards have limited impact on behavior if we take the results of research on the preaching of honesty seriously. People who know about a moral standard may or may not apply it. For example, University of Chicago researchers Hugh Hartshorne and Mark May conducted a series of studies during the 1920s strongly indicating that given the right opportunity, most people would lie, cheat, or steal if they thought they could get away with it. Variations of their study have shown the same results, whether the experimental groups were Boy Scouts or Sunday School classes. Consequently, according to Hartshorne and May's research, people act either honestly or dishonestly depending upon how they view the situation. However, as Johns Hopkins psychology professor Robert Hogan has observed, values and morals vary according to a number of factors, including the person's degree of socialization, ethical principles, and sense of autonomy. For example, a person with a strong sense of personal dignity would not face much conflict in a situation where he could steal—it would not fit his self-concept to steal. Acting in congruence with his sense of personal dignity, he would not feel frustrated because he missed an opportunity to steal and get away with it.

Knowledge of conventional morality does not predict that a person will act morally. Most convicted felons could give correct answers to questions on a test of moral knowledge but don't put the principles to practice.

If teaching and preaching do not by themselves promote so-called moral behavior, then what does? Scientists don't know precisely how we acquire values. Lawrence Kohlberg, a specialist in moral development, thinks that our sense of morality and the acquisition of our values follow a developmental timetable. As infants and toddlers we respond to praise and punishment. From those primitive beginnings we gradually learn to trade for what we want (I'll give you a candy bar if you give me your bubble gum) to satisfy *our* wishes—not necessarily the wishes of others. Next, we develop awareness of the rights of others and the importance of following the rules to help maintain the social order. This gives way to the recognition that most rules and laws have flexibility built into their structure and that few absolute rights and wrongs exist outside of definition. Finally, with the emergence of ethical principles our values firm up—we develop a sense of right and wrong that goes beyond simple praise and punishment, needs-gratification, rules, laws, and the concept of no absolutes. According to Kohlberg, at this highest stage we concern ourselves with issues of human dignity, justice, and other abstract ethical considerations.

However, few people evolve into the stage of ethical principles. To get to the stage of ethical principles, Kohlberg thinks, one has to successfully pass through the earlier stages—in other words, moral development evolves and grows according to a developmental sequence. Most people can function adequately at developmentally lower stages. Each stage, moreover, will have its own built-in frustrations. For example, the person who operates on the basis of rules may feel frustrated when people don't behave according to his rules.

Myths and fables can provide an understanding of this developmental process. The following myth of *The Boy and the Golden Cape* illustrates the values of trust, responsibility, and craftsmanship, as well as the qualities of judgment, perseverance, and innovativeness.

THE BOY AND THE GOLDEN CAPE

One day the sun god opened a golden staircase to the heavens and invited anyone who wished to make the climb, to pass through his portal and join him in his land of riches and peace. But first the person had to give the god a worthy gift.

A boy named Treegor watched scores of men, women, and children climb the stairs. The people, carrying baskets of fruit, coins, and fine ornaments, looked eager and happy, so he resolved to join them.

On the morning of his departure, he heard the voice of the wind whistling softly through the thistles saying: "If you hope to see the palace of the sun god, you will have to make a cape woven of the finest threads of gold and take it as an offering or you will burn to a cinder." Treegor had no knowledge of such things, so he resolved to ignore the wind's counsel. But as he started his journey he heard the wind again: "Make the golden cape!" To this the boy said, "I don't know how." And the wind answered, "Go to the forest."

The boy entered the forest and saw an old man who told him if he wanted threads of gold, he must look in the mountain brooks. The boy journeyed to the foot-hills and searched the brooks for gold. Then as the years passed, he found someone to love, married her, and with her raised a family. To earn a living, he learned to work as a carpenter, building fine furniture. And every so often he found some golden nuggets.

One day after his children had grown and his wife had passed away, a weaver stopped by his cabin and said, "I have come to help you turn your gold to thread and to show you how to weave your golden cape." The man applied what he had learned of patience and craftsmanship to what the weaver taught him and created a magnificent golden cape.

And so in his twilight years, the man began to make his journey back to the valley of the golden stairs. On his way he paused to rest and saw a boy approaching. Instinctively he knew what to say: "Go to the mountains. There you will find the gold you seek. But much more of value awaits you than gold."

VALUES, CHOICES, AND FRUSTRATIONS

Our values provide us with a set of premises to make comparisons and render judgments. Thoughtful comparisons require standards: criteria for measuring or evaluating thinking, feeling, and performing. This process of comparison and regulation constitutes a significant ongoing mental activity and has obvious advantages, such as adjusting or regulating our actions based on feedback.

Our values play a central role in how we direct our efforts. When we know what we value and what we don't, we less often frustrate ourselves due to indecisiveness. As reality therapist William Glasser observes, our sense of identity remains clear as we remain clear about our values: "People who know who they are rarely straddle the fence, but if they do, at least they know they are astride."

A vague value system can lead to chameleon decisions—taking action based upon superficially changing conditions.

DECISION MAKING

If we have a relatively clear understanding of our values and aims, we will act more decisively. In contrast, an ill-defined value system can lead to indecisiveness. For example, William James, the father of American psychology, describes how we can complicate our decisions through equivocations, indifference, impulsiveness, and false values. According to James, a person can inhibit her ability to make effective decisions because of internal deliberations that "contain endless degrees of complications." While admitting that deliberations may undergo evaluation and lead to an effective decision, he notes that sometimes we act too hastily before we have the relevant facts. As James put it: "with a certain indifferent acquiescence in a direction accidentally determined from without." Sometimes we act as if we can't sit passively by, and so we plunge ahead and act automatically just to do something. James notes that we might make a decision based upon a sense of "dreary resignation for the sake of austere and naked duty." In effect, we act on the basis of what we think others expect us to do. Each of James's four inhibitors would result in frustration.

If we understand what we value, then we can predict our future intentions and make and justify our decisions based upon that understanding. However, our values conflicts may cloud our choices.

VALUES CONFLICTS

We have values that sometimes conflict with our other values. Not uncommonly, we find ourselves at odds with ourselves.

We may frustrate ourselves when we value an easy lifestyle and simultaneously value quality. If we expend the effort to achieve that quality, we may frustrate our "easy life" value (or expose it as a false value); if we fail to build the quality we want due to taking it easy, then we may frustrate our quest for quality.

Two desirable values may conflict. For example, we may value honesty and simultaneously value not hurting others. Conceivably, we could get into a situation where if we spoke our honest feelings about a friend's art work, the friend would feel defeated and hurt, and we would feel frustrated because we did not live up to our standard of not hurting others. So we comment instead on how well the colors go together and refrain from telling her that we think her design looks primitive. Thus, we feel at ease with ourselves, because we think we made the right choice despite those conflicting value options. As Walt Whitman said in *Leaves of Grass*: "do I contradict myself? Very well then, I contradict myself."

At times our values appear at variance with the values of others. Some people value fashionable clothing, others value casual dress. Some value status and materialism, others value aesthetics. Some value negotiation, others value control. Mates who squabble over finances may do so because one values frugality and the other values spending. Each feels frustrated with the other during such conflicts, even though they might agree in most other respects and disagree only slightly on how much money to save.

Sometimes we don't recognize when we have a values conflict with others. We misdiagnose the problem and get involved in surface issues, such as trying to control the other person's behavior in order to achieve our ends. Identifying and clarifying our own values as well as the reasons behind our urge to control might lead to a resolution based upon judgments that bloom from a higher moral level.

POSITIVE VALUES
AND SELF-DEFEATING GOALS

At times our goals seem quite clear. However, by their very definition, we can't attain them. For example, we may value the chimeral goals of success, wealth, power, respect, approval, self-worth, control, love, comfort, meaning, or happiness.

Chimeral goals you say! How could seeking happiness, success, and meaning have anything to do with Chimera, that she-creature from Greek mythology with the lion's head, goat's body, and serpent's tail?

The creature Chimera exists only in the imagination. The goals of attaining happiness, success, and meaning have chimeric qualities if they stand suspended in the mind like a vaporous myth. Without definition, they invite frustration.

While you might value the *experiences* of happiness, success, and meaning, making them *goals* can prove both frustrating and hazardous to your mental health! For example, if they correlate with your definition of personal worth and value. When you judge your human worth on the basis of whether you feel happy, you will likely feel miserable.

L. René Gaiennie has observed that the longer people try, the harder they press, and the more they demand to achieve these fraudulent goals, the more frustrated, irritated, and inadequate they feel. He views states such as happiness, wealth, and meaning as the *results* of effective actions. You just can't wish them into existence.

People who only want success and happiness run a high risk of feeling frustrated. In contrast, the person who concentrates on developing his skills and abilities and applies them in effective ways, may produce results from his actions that have happiness, success, and meaning as by-products.

The psychologists Charles Carver and Michael Scheier believe that much human maladjustment comes when a person does not subscribe to basic values, such as the value of responsibility. People who act irresponsibly tend to get in an emotional quandary filled with frustrations. They often do not have a sense of purpose or mission in life. Such value-starved people want to feel fulfilled or likeable, but "have no idea of what actions will move them in the direction of those superordinate goals." Consequently, they will not know how to break from their ruts and often languish under the yoke of their own psychological mismanagement.

Those who seek to liberate their minds make the time to develop a sense of direction and make the effort to think and act productively. As a consequence, they create opportunities to challenge and experience themselves as relatively free from petty mental restrictions, needless fears, rigidities, fabricated helplessness, and invented depressions—the results of chimerical pranks of the mind. More importantly, they routinely experience themselves as free to experiment, to act with flexibility, to experience compassion and love, to choose what seems best, and to accept responsibility for such choices. True, those committed to this process may waver, backtrack, deny, project, and resist; *but*, they keep chipping away at the problem(s), make progress, and build upon that progress until facing challenges becomes a habit.

RESPONSIBILITY: A BASIC VALUE

Values tend to occupy a secluded place among the psychological strategies of most practicing clinicians. Values may not get center stage, although in one way or another, the counseling or psychotherapeutic process has to get involved with values whether the counselor wants to explicitly acknowledge this reality or not. So I will make no bones about it. For people to manage their frustrations effectively, they will have to act responsibly. Without a basic sense of responsibility, resolves such as "I will discipline myself to manage my frustrations" have no firm grounding. Unattached to a basic sense of responsibility, discipline is like a balloon floating in the sky. Discipline gains power when it springs from the value of assuming responsibility.

Of course, discipline may grow out of a sense of compliance. Some schoolteachers, for example, may teach discipline as a means of getting the youngsters to comply with the school routines, just as military drill instructors train soldiers to take orders without thinking. Good civilian leaders and good military officers, however, practice a discipline that grows from responsibility. In short, those who act in a responsible and disciplined fashion meet challenges, avoid procrastinating, keep out of ruts, and master their frustrations. Those trained in compliance who *believe* in acting compliantly will act accordingly. As long as someone can dictate what to do they will function. Others will not fit neatly into the responsibility-compliance dichotomy. They often won't know where they stand and will straddle the fence. They may appear behaviorally passive while very actively involved in self-contradicting thoughts. They often feel frustrated, inhibited, and stymied.

A VALUES IDENTIFICATION EXERCISE

The better you understand your values, the more likely you will master frustrations that grow from values conflicts and false goals. You can use the following values exercise to help you.

This values identification exercise breaks down into three parts:

1. Identify five prime values that you think play a central role in your behavior.
2. Specify how those values reflect in your behavior.
3. Describe how your prime values interact.

Phase one of this exercise involves identifying five of your primary values. Your challenge in this exercise involves separating socially desirable values—values that most people say they subscribe to so that they can appear good in society's eyes—from what you honestly think.

A second challenge involves resolving contradictions. Values identification and clarification may result in complications. For example, people who get irritated when delayed may think they value time because they don't want to waste their time hanging around waiting. However, people who truly value time will almost inevitably find ways of using it to their best advantage, even when faced with delays beyond their control. So we need to identify, analyze, and resolve such complications.

In completing this exercise, some readers may find they have difficulty identifying five values. If you fall into this category, don't despair. One or two basic values may suffice for this exercise. However, if you can't identify a primary value, it may mean that you will have to take time to articulate your values or your primary value may not appear on the list. If you complete this values identification exercise and discover you don't have a clear-cut system of values, you may have discovered a major source of your frustrations. You may have to search out a values system that works for you. And that will take experimentation and time, as you work your way through Kohlberg's stages of moral development. Robert Hogan, however, thinks that one need not successfully proceed through earlier stages to reach higher stages of development. Sometimes an insightful observation allows us to see new relationships between our values and behaviors that we have not experienced previously and we can leap-frog to the new standard.

Not every possible value appears on the following values list. So circle what you consider as your prime values if they appear on the list and pencil those in that don't.

1. Independence	25. Craftsmanship	49. Articulateness
2. Health	26. Knowledge	50. Forcefulness
3. Loyalty	27. Excitement	51. Determination
4. Control	28. Wisdom	52. Persistence
5. Performance	29. Inner harmony	53. Integrity
6. Appearance	30. Courage	54. Democracy
7. Money	31. Love	55. Leadership
8. Security	32. Equality	56. Responsibility
9. Competency	33. World peace	57. Competition
10. Compliance	34. Self-control	58. Innovations
11. Aesthetics	35. Identity	59. Growth
12. Freedom	36. Belonging	60. Leisure
13. Religion	37. Intuition	61. Achievement
14. Power	38. Time	62. Communication
15. Cheerfulness	39. Creativity	63. Friendship
16. Considerateness	40. Nature	64. Spirit
17. Comfort	41. Self-defense	65. Energy
18. Efficiency	42. Life	66. Family
19. Athletic ability	43. Caution	67. Recognition
20. Morality	44. Tolerance	68. Respect
21. Forgiveness	45. Compassion	69. Politeness
22. Intelligence	46. Fairness	70. Openmindedness
23. Cleanliness	47. Justice	71. Fame
24. Sex	48. Obedience	72. Honesty

Most of the listed values appear broad in scope; a few fall into a narrow category. Whether broad or narrow, each descriptive value term conveys different shades of meaning. Thus, we need to translate the term into behavior in order to determine the form, strength, and applicability of the value.

Part 2 of this exercise involves examining how your identified values translate into behavior.

Once you have identified five primary values, describe how they translate into behavior. This step will help clarify what the values mean to you and tells if you normally hold to the values you selected or have selected socially accepted ones only because they sound good. You can make up a chart similar to the following as an aid. The first entry in the chart illustrates how to do this exercise.

VALUE   BEHAVIOR

1. *Determination*   I went back to school and
                               completed a bachelor's degree
                               and . . .
                               _____
                               _____
2. _____   _____
                               _____
                               _____

After you've completed your values list, place a star beside your three most basic values. You can make that determination based upon your behavioral statements.

Part 3 of this exercise involves clarifying how your primary values interact. Values tend to fall into a sequence of relevancy in which one holds dominance over all others under most circumstances. For example, truth may seem more important than friendship under most conditions, but sometimes friendship holds more value than truth. So, first identify your priority values.

Next, network your values by visualizing how your basic values complement each other. For example, suppose you value time, helpfulness, and compassion. You might find that you would prefer to use your time in providing services to emotionally troubled humans. Thus, this network of values will give you a sense of how your prime value cluster may assert an organizing effect on your actions.

A VALUES CLARIFICATION EXERCISE

The values clarification specialist Louis Raths reformulated questions from the work of the famous educator and and psychologist John Dewey. These questions could help you gain further values clarity.

You can adapt these questions to important circumstances and less important ones as well.

1. What do I see as my alternatives?
2. What positive and/or negative consequences follow the enactment of each alternative.
3. Does the choice I make represent what I think or do I march to the tune of "someone else's drummer"?
4. Does the issue represent something very important to me?
5. Would I take a public stand on this issue?
6. Do I think I would act on the basis of this view?
7. Do I act with consistency on this issue?

The values clarification questions apply to many of our daily choices. The first two questions, in particular, can apply to almost any situation involving a decision.

To the extent that you come to understand the principles by which you operate, you free yourself to make choices that can help you change patterns that run at variance with what you stand for.

In section 3 we consider three areas pregnant with potential frustrations—managing people, careers, and time. While values clarification concepts apply to each, I do not include specific values exercises in the following chapters. However, you can translate your values identification and clarification work from this chapter to each situation. You can also apply change and problem-solving concepts. For example, if you normally master your frustrations with frustrating people and your career and steer away from procrastinating, what values do you think translate into these competencies? How do you view the changes you go through as you seek mastery in interpersonal communications, career direction, and time management? What problem-solving strategies do you use to obtain the results you seek?

PART III

LIFE FRUSTRATIONS

In this part, we will examine three universal frustrations: coping with difficult people, with our careers, and with procrastination; and we will consider practical problem-solving approaches for dealing with each condition.

Practically everyone confronts people who prove frustrating. In Chapter 7 we will look at people who frustrate us and what we can do. Chapter 8 concentrates on career frustrations; specifically, why most people feel dissatisfied with their work and what they can do to ease their frustrations and gain work satisfaction. To move this process along, we consider a career review and how to employ rational career management. Chapter 9 addresses a truly universal habit: procrastination. Through this chapter you can find ways to recognize your own procrastination problem, learn how this frustrating habit develops, and learn how to use tested counterprocrastination tactics.

CHAPTER SEVEN

MANAGING FRUSTRATING PEOPLE

Have you ever gotten so frustrated with someone that you felt like pulling your hair out and screaming? For example, your employee acts as if she didn't hear your instructions, even after you repeated yourself. The parts supply person won't look for that very inexpensive but vital part you need. Your depressive neighbor comes over unannounced to moan about her problems. The coach of your child's Little League team rarely lets your child play, though your child has proven himself as a fine player in a more difficult league. You invite a couple you have not seen for years as weekend guests and he leaves water rings on your flawless mahogany table, and she drops cigarette ashes on your rug.

You would have a rare tolerance (or spend your time denying reality) if you did not occasionally find someone's actions frustrating.

WHO FRUSTRATES WHOM?

We get frustrated when we deal with other people we think block, thwart, impede, or interrupt us. We all know people who frustrate us, but do they think *we* frustrate *them*?

For example, an employer may complain about an employee's poor work habits. In the next room, the frustrated employee complains about his employer's inability to communicate what he wants done. A civil servant complains to a colleague about a demanding and frustrating taxpayer. And the taxpayer talks to her friends about how she felt frustrated by the bureaucrat's sluggish pace and surly manner.

Most people normally do not go out of their way to act in a difficult and frustrating manner. Nevertheless, interpersonal frustrations arise when we see people acting against our wishes, expectations, and values.

In the following pages, we will consider three sources of people frustrations, five types of frustrating people, and a seven-point plan for mastering interpersonal frustrations. The three sources include conflicts of interest, personality clashes, and unfairness. The five types include tyrants, constructives, spectators, neurotics, and normals. The seven-point plan provides a blueprint for limiting people frustrations and identifying and preventing avoidable clashes. Let's start with conflicts of interests.

CONFLICTS OF INTEREST

Most legitimate frustration problems arise when one person's self-interests clash with the interests of another. For example, such conflicts of interest can occur between people who wait in line and those who cut ahead in line, between nations with competitive economic positions, between companies marketing similar products, as well as between different departments within an organization.

Conflicts of interest often occur between family members. Let's use the case of Sally and Jack as an illustration.

Sally decides that she wants to start a clean-up campaign and wants her six-year-old son, Jack, to clean up his room. So she insists that Jack go clean his room. But he wants to watch his favorite TV cartoon show and balks. Both Sally and Jack have plans they don't want to interrupt. A clash of interests will occur unless they recognize how to cope with the problem by first not exaggerating it.

Dramatizing a conflict of interests often helps escalate it. Let's look at the case of Bob and Amber for an example of this conflict-escalation process.

Bob wants to take the family to the mountains for their vacation, but Amber says she dislikes the mountains and wants to go to the shore. The conflict of interests intensifies as Amber locks onto the idea that Bob should realize that she doesn't want to spend her valuable vacation time in some desolate, dark, and dusty cabin shrouded in damp, chilly, mountain air. This mind-set against the mountains leads to an escalation of the dispute when she thinks Bob behaves especially unfairly by planning such a trip. This process builds up steam when each frustrates the other by quarreling and stewing. In actuality, neither wants to hassle the other. Instead, the person just wants to do what he or she wants to do.

Managing Conflicts of Interest   As implied in the cases of Sally and Jack and Bob and Amber, one potent solution to conflicts of interests involves compromise. Bob and Amber, for example, may compromise by having their vacation at a mountain lake resort.

A more basic solution to dealing with conflicts of interests begins with recognizing our vital self-interests. The more you know about your self-interest, especially vital interests, the more likely you will recognize potential conflict points in your transactions with others and can choose to prevent avoidable clashes. We know, for instance, that most sensible people want to maintain a good self-image. A conflict arises if that image gets challenged. A conflict will also arise if one's income gets threatened. People will normally see a potential loss of income as a threat to their interests. However, if you want your mate to fix you a sandwich and she balks, such actions may not constitute a vital conflict of interests.

What do you consider your vital interests? Maintaining your key relationships, job, property, family safety, and personal dignity might qualify. With some thought, most people can identify their major interests. Identifying such interests has value in that once we get them into sharp focus, we will have a better understanding of what we want to protect and why.

Knowing our vital self-interests helps us avoid conflicts over pseudo-issues and instead puts our energies to work doing what will help us the most.

An analysis of possible points of conflict can yield important ideas concerning how to minimize frustrations. I'll use a consulting situation to illustrate this point. When I put on my cap as a management consultant, I will occasionally help break a new manager in to his or her position. As one of my practices, I will help identify conflicts of interests between this person and other managers. On one such occasion, I asked a newly appointed manager to try to identify potential conflicts of interests that could affect his relations with other department heads. At first he said that his colleagues worked together as a team to achieve a common goal. A careful analysis of potential points of conflict, however, showed that he had overlapping responsibilities with other department heads concerning use of floating laborers, demands for maintenance services, transportation of materials, and so forth. Such overlapping responsibilities could, if improperly managed, adversely impact his budgetary results which, in turn, could affect the security of his job and/or his remuneration. An in-depth evaluation of his situation made this clear, and he quickly learned that the other departmental heads would act within their budgetary interest and some of their actions could frustrate his interests.

To reduce these points of conflict I recommended ways to improve coordination of functions and minimize conflicts of interests. However, some remained, and the manager had to learn to balance his budgetary interests with those of other managers and still work to achieve corporate goals.

PERSONALITY CLASHES

Some people naturally seem to clash. For example, Tom thinks the new shop foreman comes from the Simian period, when monkeys and apes reigned. "He's crude," Tom thinks, "I don't think he fits in with the rest of us. I really can't tolerate being around him." Dan, the new foreman, thinks: "That Tom is a pansy. He has no guts. I'll bet he spends his spare time making paper dolls." It seems clear that they do not like each other. Historically, we have called this a personality clash.

No law says we have to like everyone. Indeed, we will find it difficult to relate to some people if we can't find common interests. Furthermore, some individuals have traits that turn us off. We may not like pushy salespeople or people who won't stand up and express their true feelings. Also, we might have an aversion to people we view as loud and arrogant. Yet most people with qualities we don't like know others who care for them, and so they must possess at least a few good qualities.

Interventions to Reduce Personality Clashes   Sometimes it helps to understand what you dislike about a person you have a strong negative reaction toward, especially if you can't avoid this person— a coworker, neighbor, subordinate, customer, or employer. You could profit from objectively defining the person's less desirable traits as well as his salvageable qualities. For example, you don't like your coworker Alvin. So you decide to analyze the reasons, using the following questions:

1. Does he dress oddly?
2. Does his voice sound offensive? If so, how?
3. Do his facial features or hairstyle bother me?
4. Do I find his movements or mannerisms peculiar?
5. What do I know about his values? How do they seem to align with my primary values?
6. Does he exhibit some traits I don't like, such as lateness, loudness, or arrogance?
7. Does he seem to communicate on a different wave length: different interests, concerns, priorities?
8. Did he grow up in a different socioeconomic environment?
9. Does he look unappealing? If so, how?
10. Does he act manipulatively: like a victim?
11. Do some of his traits or qualities remind me of ones I don't like in myself?
12. Does he remind me of somebody I have had conflicts with?
13. Does he act too competitively?
14. Do his actions cause me additional work?
15. Does he try to bully me?

By getting specific about what you dislike about Alvin, you can better combat the problem that exists within you, as well as the problem you think the person causes for you.

Now try to broaden your view of Alvin to see him in a favorable light. For example, what three factors do you like most about this person? How would you view him if he knew an important person you wanted to know?

You have other ways to diminish your negative reaction to the Alvins of the world. For example, you might try to adopt a professional attitude by viewing your transactions with them as part of the job of coexisting.

Suppose you have carefully and fairly analyzed the reasons why Alvin does not appeal to you and for good reason you'd prefer to avoid him. You might figure out ways to reduce your exposure to him.

UNFAIRNESS AND FRUSTRATION

We've all met people who frustrate us by impeding our goals without just cause. At the least, we feel frustrated when this happens. Such "unfairnesses" take many personal as well as impersonal forms: we have multiple troubles; we get falsely accused; we don't get our way; someone takes advantage of us; it "rains on our parade"; we receive a parking citation just before we put the coin in the meter; or a friend has an affair with our mate. Clearly, when we view a situation as unfair, we probably will feel frustrated. Since we don't have to look far to find examples of unfairness, we could find much to feel frustrated about.

Webster's New Collegiate Dictionary defines *unfairness* as having to do with dishonest or deceptive activities. In daily practice, unfair has come to mean much more than that—anything that cuts across the grain of our values, wishes, or expectations.

In the section that follows, we'll look into our options for managing frustrations due to unfairness.

MANAGING UNFAIRNESS

A key phrase to managing unfairness involves validating our perceptions of that unfair situation. Admittedly, we may find this validation process difficult, especially if we feel frustrated over the thought of the impediment. So we call upon ourselves to perception-check in the midst of a disruptive experience. When we perception-check, we try to discriminate between sound and unsound assumptions.

We take assumptions for granted. We assume, for example, that the sun will not burn out tomorrow. We have great confidence in this assumption because it fits with past experiences and scientifically valid predictions. However, assumptions such as "I should be treated fairly" often prove unsound. In this regard Albert Ellis has wisely noted: "there is no law in the universe that says things *should* be fair. It would be nice if life were the way we wished, but we can't count on such wishes coming true."

Sometimes we assume that because we feel intensely about a situation, our intensity validates our perception. Emotional intensity, however, does not validate the perception. For example, a paranoid person who thinks the rabbit in his backyard spies on him and reports to the president of the United States may have intense feelings. But the delusion only serves to intensify the feeling.

We can't always change an unfair person's behavior however hard we try. But we do have the potential to reshape our attitudes and behavior toward people whose traits, behavior, or appearance we don't like, so as not to add to our frustrations, conflicts, and disadvantages. We can partially accomplish this by asking and thoughtfully answering questions such as: What makes him so important that I feel compelled to ruminate over his less desirable traits and behaviors?

WHO PROVES MOST FRUSTRATING?

In this section we will consider five types of people whose actions can impede our progress and consider what we can do to manage our transactions with them. The five types include the tyrant, constructive, spectator, neurotic, and "normal." This section reflects a collaborative effort with the psychologist and business consultant, L. René Gaiennie.

The Ancient Tyrannical Process As a young child, Sylvia accompanied her physician-father to the hospital on Saturdays, where she watched him perform autopsies on one or more of his weekly surgery cases. Then they would return to their cluttered Victorian home, morbidly decorated in hues of brown, black, and gray. And over a candlelit supper, she and her family would talk of death and dying.

Over the years Sylvia developed a certin callousness toward life, a whiny self-serving disposition, and an urge to destroy. She had a high need to achieve, but her omnipresent subtle, manipulative style caused most people to avoid her. Her destructive manner, her father's unpopularity with his peers, and her marginal college grades resulted in repeated failures to gain admission to medical school.

Embittered by her inability to gain acceptance to medical school, she pursued an introverted young medical student and persuaded him to marry her.

By the age of thirty, Sylvia had twice married. Her first husband became impotent with her and left her for a male lover. The second committed suicide.

I first met Sylvia when she came to therapy with her new male lover, Peter, who initiated therapy because of an impotency problem he started to develop with her. Sylvia had strongly opposed involving a third party, but when Peter said he would go to counseling on his own, she came along to protect her interests.

Sylvia exemplified the ancient tyrannical process. In this timeless progression, the tyrant, swamped by dissatisfactions and repressed energies, directs his efforts to manipulate, coerce, and control others. Driven by preservation fears, insecurities, and hostility, this person's actions ultimately prove destructive, because insightfulness and creativity get invested in an organized life plan of pressuring and coercing others in order that the tyrant may prevail. Believing that only victory brings power, the tyrant fears the tenuousness of power and does what she can to keep it.

Not all tyrannical people act on the basis of fear and control. Some psychopathic types try to manipulate others through charm. Their uninhibited and superficially friendly manner can prove quite disarming. They have no social conscience and no compunction to take what you have and make it theirs. They don't care how they do it.

You can best cope with tyrants and psychopaths by recognizing them and then by keeping away from them. Taking time to rehabilitate them often proves self-defeating and adds to your frustrations. They rarely change.

The Constructive Person   Like the tyrant, the constructive individual uses insights, intuition, analysis, planning, and organizing ability to achieve results. But the results reflect expansion and progression, not constriction and coercion.

People who creatively dedicate themselves to their projects concentrate most of their attention on them. As long as they remain involved with the project, you may find them frustrating to deal with, especially if you ask them to do something they have little interest in doing.

The highly focused efforts of constructive people can place a strain on their personal relations. The person may not take enough time to participate in activities with the significant people in his or her life.

Constructive people don't necessarily prove universally efficient. For example, some constructive idea people prove weak on follow-through. They develop the idea and then avoid completing the project. Once they conceive the idea, the constructive person's interests may diminish.

In dealing with constructives, we do better when we display tolerance for their style. We may even want to encourage it or help out with follow-through efforts, as required.

To maintain good communications with constructives it helps to recognize the value of their contributions—even if you disagree with them. On the other hand, if you agree, then encourage them.

Constructives typically respond better to challenges. So if you create positive challenges for these individuals, they will tend to respond productively.

The Spectator Spectators made the discovery that members of the audience seem to live more comfortable lives than the players. This dysfunctional insight causes them to display a sense of ineptitude as the two following case examples suggest.

Alan did the minimum required both at home and at work. He just didn't want to get involved. He feared that doing well would cause others to give him more work and responsibility. Elizabeth, another spectator, made a zero contribution to her hiking club.

The Alans and Elizabeths of the world can frustrate us, because we can't count on them.

Clear communications can often remedy many frustrating situations with unresponsive spectators. Indeed, some spectators respond quite well when you say what you want in a factual, non-condemning, tolerant but firm manner. While objective communications can clear up ambiguity, don't expect miracles. This group does not yield easily to change.

If you want to make some headway, however, you will have to figure out a way to cause them to take action. Having the spectator agree to a project and to meeting a schedule sometimes helps, as does taking the lead and getting them to work along with you. Both strategies, however, require follow-up efforts on your part.

The Neurotic The neurotic often proves frustrating to relate to because he tends to display rigidity, dogmatism, and low frustration tolerance in his interpersonal dealings.

Rigid people with low frustration tolerance often prove quite difficult to deal with. They resist efforts to change.

Stubborn individuals, know-it-alls, malcontents, depressives, love lushes, the inhibited, the phobic, the narcissistic, whiners and complainers, hostile and aggressive individuals, and people who play one-upmanship games all fall into this neurotic category. The hyperactive boss running about screaming and putting down his subordinates falls into this category as does the nice guy who can act just wonderful as well as whimpering and weak-willed.

Neurotics may overreact, get defensive, or misconstrue our intentions. Because of strong tendencies to distort reality, they prove difficult and frustrating to deal with.

Some neurotics try to compensate for their disturbance by sticking to the strictest interpretation of the rules. This attitude can prove annoying if we find them in a position of authority and we want some minor rules changed in order to accomplish our objectives.

While most people try to resolve their interpersonal problems amicably, neurotics place emphasis upon control rather than negotiation to get things done. Their controlling compulsion could frustrate our constructive intentions.

The following five-point plan applies to handling neurotic individuals.

1. Don't take neurotic behavior personally. You will probably see that others have similar problems with that individual.
2. Few people find disturbed behavior agreeable. Even the person who acts disturbed probably would change the behavior if he could. So

try to look beyond the symptom and understand that you may have real limitations in your dealings with that troubled person.

3. Be clear, firm, and specific in your communications.

4. Enlist the person's support, if possible, to help you find an alternative way to solve your problem. Most neurotic individuals would prefer to have your approval than to feel alienated. They may harden their position if they view your actions as threatening their security.

5. You may find that you simply can't get your ideas across. Under such circumstances, try to find someone else to deal with.

The "Normal" Our most frequent frustrations come from our dealings with so-called normal people.

"Normals" can act like toned-down tyrants, constructives, spectators, and neurotics. When under stress, some of their less favorable traits will blossom. Fortunately, normals have more flexibility than neurotics, more energy than spectators, more time than constructives, and don't have life-destruction plans like tyrants. They also will tend to act more sensibly compared to neurotics, who tend to operate according to highly personalized motives.

If we don't have a major personality clash with someone, we can usually find a way to negotiate differences and come to some resolution of our frustrations in our dealings with him. The following seven-point plan may apply when dealing with another person with whom you are having a problem.

1. Get clear on the issue.
2. Articulate the problem.
3. Involve the person in mutual problem solving.
4. Keep your tone of voice and contemplated actions *positive*.
5. Consider palatable alternatives.
6. Reinforce positive contributions.
7. Articulate the final plan and get agreement.

In your dealings with normals (as well as with neurotics, spectators, and constructives) strive to act trustworthy. People who don't trust you could frustrate your positive intentions and goals.

Most people like to know they can count on what you say. This trust takes time to build, generally proves mutual, and reduces the risk of misunderstandings that could polarize a relationship and make a not-so-difficult person frustratingly difficult.

WHAT YOU CAN DO TO MASTER YOUR
FRUSTRATIONS ABOUT FRUSTRATING PEOPLE

If you know your vital interests and have a constructive purpose, frustrating people normally stand only as temporary impediments. As long as you know what you want to accomplish, you actually might turn most people to your side. The following self-management strategies may apply when dealing with your own frustrations about the actions of others.

1. Recognize the two sides of every story.
2. Try to anticipate and prevent avoidable conflicts and frustrations by using effective problem-solving methods.
3. Look beyond the immediate frustration and determine what you really want to accomplish.
4. Articulate, in clear terms, what you want or will accept.
5. React positively and firmly.
6. Strive to establish mutual trust.
7. Recognize limitations.

CHAPTER EIGHT

MANAGING YOUR CAREER FRUSTRATIONS

In the story of the grasshopper and the ant, the playful grasshopper fiddled his summer away and found himself ill-prepared for the winter. The hard-working ant, on the other hand, spent his summer stowing away food. For all his hard work, the ant appeared as a rather colorless character compared to the flamboyant grasshopper. But he survived!

We work to survive. If our work gives us opportunities for experiencing fulfillment, so much the better. If we can balance our work with pleasurable and enjoyable outside activities, better yet. If we can do that and blend the favorable qualities of both the grasshopper and the ant in our daily work, best yet.

Blending our grasshopper and ant tendencies into our work provides a vehicle for survival, learning, material gain, and psychological fulfillment. These four factors alone point out the importance of rationally positioning oneself to do the right kind of work (whatever that may involve). However, other practical reasons exist that point to career development as an important undertaking.

The average person over the course of his or her lifetime will shift careers three to five times. Some of these shifts result from necessity (one gets fired or the company goes bankrupt). Some shifts grow from changing interests or competencies. Some from expediency and poor planning (accepting a job offer without relating one's interests and abilities to the job description), resulting in performing functions one does not like to do.

Biological scientist Hans Selye points out that repeatedly performing undesired work functions can promote harmful stress. You can avoid this stress by selecting a work environment "which is in line with your innate preferences—to find an activity you like and respect." He goes on to say, "Only thus can you eliminate the need for frustrating constant readaptation that is the major cause of stress."

Unfortunately, many of us find ourselves tied to careers in which we perform tedious, unpleasant, and frustrating activities. Indeed, our more dismal career satisfaction statistics portray 80 percent of us as frustrated with our careers. So if you find yourself in that category, you have an important challenge to find a career pathway you can respect—one where you perform functions you enjoy and can do well. In other words, you need to look at how to get control of your career direction and invest in turning career frustrations into challenges and opportunities. However, if you have already joined the ranks of those who truly enjoy what they do, then you may want to read this chapter to gather some ideas on how to add more enjoyment to your work. The system I present in this chapter suggests how to do this. It describes career reviews and how to make them, the value of learning through experimenting, and rational career management.

WHY MAKE A CAREER REVIEW?

Job satisfaction ranks high as an important goal, but most people think they experience less work satisfaction than they would like. Consequently, they will periodically question the values and meaning of what they do and wonder if they haven't missed out on something better. A good career review allows one to look objectively into this question and may show sources of career satisfaction previously ignored, new career pathways, or the wisdom of maintaining your current career track. Normally, we have three basic reasons for conducting a career review:

1. *Lifestyle changes:* Each stage of life creates different demands, such as adolescent identity confusion, mid-life career shifts, work

force reentry for mothers after child-rearing, preretirement concerns, and retirement careers.

2. *Changing opportunities:* Hundreds of new career opportunities open yearly and others shut down. Technical changes in the form of computer technology and robotics already have started to open new career opportunities.

3. *Career evolution:* We don't work toward some master career goal. Instead we evolve in our career direction due to changing conditions, surprise opportunities, and unexpected changes. We need to prepare ourselves to recognize and meet such challenges.

The three motives point to the importance of considering your age and physical condition, mental ability, and behavior flexibility in your career review. As noted in Chapter 1, we have control over building our bodies, liberating our minds, and changing our patterns. However, we have limitations as to how far we can stretch these changes in developing our careers. A small, frail person, for example, would have a hard time working as a lumberjack. A basketball player would have trouble getting a part as a Munchkin in *The Wizard of Oz.*

THE CAREER REVIEW

In this section we will consider six major parts to a career review:

- Reasons for career frustrations
- A productive point of view
- The six conditions for work satisfaction
- Three basic career dimensions
- Career trade-offs
- How to expand your career review

Reasons for Career Frustrations   Some career frustrations prove inevitable. After all, we can't always have our way, we often get interrupted when we least want to, and we sometimes lack information that could make our work run smoothly.

Occasionally we snare ourselves in a career frustration that results from faulty ideas and expectations. Sometimes these frustrations build up and lead to burnout. Many of the characteristics of the burnout group occur in lesser degree with people who work at tasks they don't like but only marginally tolerate. By examining this more extreme sample of career stress victims, we can spotlight some of the factors underlying career frustrations.

"Burnouts" experience their work as an endless frustration and strain. They reach the burnout point when their job frustrations overflow because of one or more of the following reasons:

1. Unrealistic work expectations
2. Perceived lack of control
3. Interests, values, or abilities that fail to match the job requirements
4. Too few common interests with coworkers, superiors, subordinates, or customers
5. Overconscientiousness

Instead of working to make improvements or changes in their careers, many succumb to their own defenses—rigidly stick to the organization's rules, stay out of work because of headaches and other stress symptoms, misuse drugs or alcohol, escape through gambling, cause trouble, or engage in other self-defeating activities. Sometimes burnouts become noticeably depressed or agitated and put their efforts into protecting themselves from losing control rather than in seeking mastery by finding a work atmosphere that suits them. When a person tries to avoid losing control, he or she will often defensively seek shelter as an agoraphobic seeks shelter by staying at home out of fear of the outside world. To break this pattern, a productive and radical shift in emphasis can help.

A Productive Point of View   When you get involved in preferred career activities, you add fulfillment to your pay check. Unfortunately, sometimes we block ourselves from visualizing careers that give us the option to do what we do best. We shroud those options and defeat our constructive purposes when we turn inward and focus upon dissatisfactions instead of upon opportunities. In contrast, visualizing what we can accomplish in the right career for us allows for a productive shift in emphasis.

L. René Gaiennie has mapped out the contrasts between self-centered preoccupations and action alternatives that point to the importance of thinking productively and keeping flexible. The following chart describes his approach.

INDEX

C

Lewin, Kurt, 14
Lilliputians, 3
Listening skills
  description of, 40
  prescription for improving, 40
Low frustration tolerance
  ABC method and, 34–35
  advantages of overcoming
    frustration disturbances, 28
  bi-directional process and, 21
  biological tendencies and, 22,
    29
  boredom and, 39
  breaking problem habits and,
    27
  case examples of, 19–21
  common threads and, 20
  condemning others and, 39
  control and, 35
  definition, 18
  depression and, 38–39
  discomfort dodging and, 21–22
  disturbance and, 24–25
  enigmatic quality of, 29
  fear of disapproval and, 38
  fear of self-assertion and, 41
  feeling rushed and, 36
  frustration tolerance training
    and, 16
  impatience and, 34
  impulsiveness and, 34
  intrasensory information and,
    31–32
  inventory, 33–34
  language and, 25
  laziness and, 28
  listening skills and, 44
  neurosis and, 100
  overreactions and, 36
  perfectionism and, 23–24
  pouting and, 41–42
  problem habits and, 26–27, 39–
    40
  procrastination and, 37
  ruts and, 37–38
  self-concept and, 25–26
  self-defeating effects of, 56

  speaking skills and, 40–41
  stubbornness and, 41
  sulking, and, 41–42
  symptoms of, 19–20, 24–27
  type A personality and, 20–21
  urgency and, 34
  See also Frustration causes.
Luria, A. R., 25

M

Maier, Norman R.F., 66
Management, See Frustration
    management techniques.
Mañana diversion, 127–28
May, Mark, 76
McDougal, William, 108
McGill University study, 10
Meichenbaum, Donald, 56–57
Montgomery, Robert, 50
Moral development
  autonomy and, 77
  Hogan's views of, 78
  Kohlberg's views of, 77–78
  stages of, 77–78, 84

N

Necessity of failure concept, 50–
    53, 59
Needing framework, 56
Neff, Walter, 116
Neurotics, 100–101
Newton, Isaac, 126
Normals, 101

O

Obsessive ruminations, 26
Odyssey and problem solving, 62
Osborn, A. F., 72
Overreactions
  description of, 36
  prescriptions for, 36

P

Paradigm shift, 64
Paradoxes

Getting creatively involved in results-oriented activities involves changing

FROM	TO
Insistence upon success	Willingness to risk failure
Constraints	Freedom
Problems	Opportunities
Finding ourselves	Losing ourselves in goal-directed activities
Risk avoidance	Risk management
Reducing the malfunctional	Expanding the functional
Need fulfillment	Using failures to spur the development of improved methods, procedures, and so forth.
Old boundaries	New insights
Demands on others	Personal resourcefulness
Inaction	Action
Dependency	Self-sustaining behavior
Emphasis upon needs	Emphasis upon problem solving

Gaiennie goes on to say that a strong shift in orientation from self-centered activities toward action alternatives creates a series of paradoxes including

1. Attention to detailed relationships *and* interest in
   novelty
   flux
   change
   improvisation
2. Desire to organize *and* willingness to withstand the lack of
   structure
   control
   immediate results
   predictability
3. Liking orderliness *and* tolerance for
   ambiguity
   uncertainty
   play and humor
   complexity
   risk
   being and feeling different

4. Willingness to listen *and* willingness to
   make independent judgments
   separate source from content
   suspend judgments

The paradoxes produce a *balance* and their natural coexistence sets the stage for acting with firm flexibility (we feel firm in what we want but flexible enough to change) in our career and personal activities.

The Six Conditions for Work Satisfaction   The concept of the balance between opposites sets the stage for looking into six more specific factors that relate to work satisfaction. The following describes these six factors.

1. Purposeful and Productive Work
William McDougall, one of America's early psychological thinkers, organized his psychology around the theory that the individual gains greatest satisfaction when engaged in purposeful activities. People who seem to enjoy what they do view their efforts as purposeful, productive, and leading to something. Their work provides them with a sense of accomplishment.

2. The Right Level
The Peter Principle states that some people rise to the level of their incompetency. However, many people fail to rise to the level of their competency due to misconceptions, lack of information, psychological inhibition, failure to see opportunities, failure to test out new opportunities, self-doubts, low frustration tolerance, fear of change, and so forth.

    People who find themselves underemployed (functioning well below their competency level) or overemployed (in over their heads) usually have much to feel frustrated about. Marked disparities between abilities and performance prove a major source of frustrations. Ideally, when your abilities harmonize with the job functions, you will enjoy what you do and will have less reason to feel frustrated.

3. Enjoyable Work Functions
Preferred work functions seem to get priority treatment, and the person seems to exhibit enjoyment while performing them. The

salesperson, for example, who prefers to serve as a customer's "consultant" will appear more involved when talking to the customer about how to improve the products display than when giving a hard sell or filling out a call report.

We rarely find a person who enjoys all functions of a particular job. Some people like to do research but don't like to write up the results. Some people like to write reports but don't like to gather the data that go into the report. Some people like customer contact work but don't like to make the phone calls to set up the contact. Some people like most facets of their jobs but some more than others. The opportunity to perform more of the preferred than unpreferred job functions correlates with greater job satisfaction.

4. A Sense of Competency

People with good work skills who work to upgrade those skills generally find greater job satisfaction than those with weak skills. As a person develops skill, he frees himself from the uncertainty, awkwardness, and frustration inherent in the learning process and frees his mind to concentrate on higher levels of accomplishment. For example, the person who first learns to ski falls many times before mastering the skills necessary to negotiate the expert slopes. Having the skills enables him to concentrate upon traversing that expert ski slope, not upon splinter skills or upon self-observation.

5. Common Interests and Values

Most occupations attract people with roughly similar values and/ or interest patterns. People whose values and interests do not align well with the values and interests of their coworkers risk added frustrations. For example, a nondrinking sensitive writer may find it difficult to relate to hard-drinking colleagues in an advertising agency.

6. Temperamental Suitability

A person's temperament may determine his job choice. If disparities exist between his disposition and work responsibilities, then frustration can result from the disparity. A shy person, for example, likely would find it hard to perform well as a store security guard.

Summing up, those who get the most out of their work generally do something they consider purposeful and productive, operate at the right level, perform functions they enjoy, exhibit competency for what they do, deal on a daily basis with people with whom they have common interests and values, and seem temperamentally suited to their work.

Career Dimensions   The six factors for career satisfaction provide criteria for making a career choice, but other criteria exist that merit consideration, such as the accompanying comparative career dimensions.

TO APPLY PERSONAL QUALITIES TO CAREER CONDITIONS

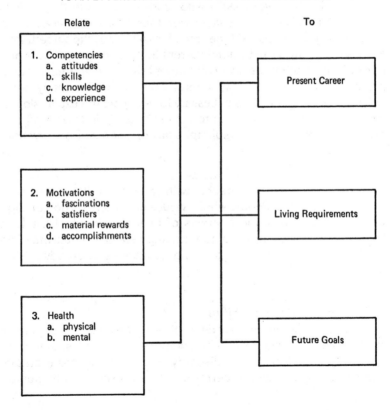

Relate   To

1. Competencies
   a. attitudes
   b. skills
   c. knowledge
   d. experience

Present Career

2. Motivations
   a. fascinations
   b. satisfiers
   c. material rewards
   d. accomplishments

Living Requirements

3. Health
   a. physical
   b. mental

Future Goals

In completing this analysis, relate your competencies, motivations, and health to your present career, living requirements, and future goals. Then question to what extent the variables on the left side of the page fit with the dimensions on the right side of the page. If you find only rough correspondence between both sides of the ledger, you may have to weigh the pros and cons of your analysis in order to clarify disparities. For example, let's suppose you work as a dentist. You have the competency to do your job expertly. Your present work provides the financial resources to enjoy driving a luxury automobile, for sending your youngsters to good private schools, and for living in an upper-middle-income neighborhood. However, you've lost fascination for your work and experience fewer work satisfactions. Furthermore, you feel mildly depressed about your future, as the dental field gets congested with new practitioners. You think you need to spark up your career and add excitement and opportunities to your routine. But first you decide what trade-offs you'd consider making.

Career Trade-Offs   In the above analysis, you matched your competencies, motivations, and health factors against your present career choice or job experience, living requirements, and future career and personal goals. You can now expand your career assessment by exploring career trade-offs.

As you consider the relationships described in the section on comparative career dimensions, you also can consider several important trade-offs. Does your career provide you with an adequate income? Does your career afford you opportunities to actualize your interests? Does your career offer high risks and high rewards vs. low risks and predictable rewards? Does it allow you to travel or stay in one place? Do you have career relations with people whom you value? Do you live in an area you prefer? Do you have time for hobbies, friends, exercise, and relaxation? Do you have opportunities to advance your wisdom and expertise? Does your career allow for adjustments depending upon your life stage: youth, young adult, maturity, old age? Do you have the willingness and resources to pay the admission price to get into a new career or to advance in your present career?

In examining the trade-offs, the views of mature and sensible people can often help bring your career evaluation into sharper perspective. If you choose to seek counsel, keep yourself responsible for your decisions. A willingness to make yourself accountable for your decisions adds to the value of such a discussion.

How to Expand Your Career Review You can use one or a combination of the following ways to refine your career review: 1. bootstrap programs, 2. vocational testing, 3. enjoyable work experience analysis, 4. Terkel's three basic questions, 5. job function analysis, and 6. special publications and handbooks.

Vocational bootstrap programs exist where you follow career identification guidelines and do-it-yourself programs. Richard Bolle's book *What Color Is Your Parachute?* contains many worthwhile ideas that you can use to help define your interests and competencies and refine your career goals. However, certain career guidance tests, such as the *Strong Campbell Interest Inventory*; measures of traits and temperament, such as *The Sixteen Personality Factor Questionnaire*; and a good aptitude test battery, such as the *General Aptitude Test Battery* (usually administered at your state employment office) may prove of greater benefit. They can provide a broad overview of possible career directions and help you narrow your search.

Many fine vocational tests exist that can provide fruitful information concerning career selection or a career shift. A standard battery of vocational tests, including measures of interests, personal preferences, values, temperament, personality, and aptitudes can prove useful in identifying *potential* career directions. Follow-up readings about the suggested occupations, talking to people employed in the target occupation(s), and some type of job review (voluntary work, part-time work, education, special seminars, on-the-job training, and so forth), often help determine a viable career direction.

Many colleges and universities offer vocational testing and career planning services at reasonable fees. Using such a service may prove an inexpensive and possibly effective way to get started.

You can help yourself identify career possibilities through listing your five most enjoyable work experiences, then analyzing these experiences using a few basic questions:

- What conditions surrounded those experiences?
- What phases of the experience proved most challenging?

- What outcomes resulted from each of the experiences?
- What common threads pull through the experiences?

Studs Terkel in his book *Working* related three basic questions relevant to the issue of career review:

- What do I do during the day?
- What do I think about doing it?
- What do I feel about doing it?

Such questions often can provide clues concerning interests and abilities. For example, a receptionist may prefer handling problem inquiries compared to routing calls. Since problem-solving opportunities rarely occur and phone calls seem almost continuous, this person spends more time doing what she doesn't like instead of doing what she likes.

If she listens to what she tells herself about the work and identifies both desirable and undesirable activities, she may develop a clearer career picture. For example, she may discover an interest in analyzing the callers' personalities or moods.

Moreover, the receptionist can carry this inquiry one step further by probing the question of what specifically she likes about handling problem inquiries.

The following inventory presents general functions you might like or dislike performing. To use the job function inventory, first evaluate each function according to your degree of interest in the function and your potential to perform it.

	INTEREST High/Med./Low	ESTIMATED POTENTIAL High/Med./Low
1. Working with ideas		
2. Analyzing problems		
3. Working with mechanical objects		
4. Making decisions		
5. Preparing reports		
6. Conducting research		
7. Answering complaints		
8. Managing crises		

	INTEREST High/Med./Low	ESTIMATED POTENTIAL High/Med./Low
9. Filing and typing		
10. Entertaining others		
11. Talking to people		
12. Trying out new experiences		
13. Problem solving		
14. Negotiating contracts		
15. Competitive situations		
16. Scheduling		
17. Managing money		
18. Helping others		
19. Planning and organizing		
20. Using farm machinery		
21. Working with tools		
22. Fixing things		
23. Analyzing the stock market		
24. Defending people's rights		
25. Attending to the medical needs of others		
26. Commercial activities		
27. Artistic activities		
28. Musical activities		
29. Public broadcasting		
30. Photographic work		
31. Teaching		
32. Fund raising		

Since hundreds of vocational possibilities exist, the list only scratches the surface of possible functions. However, you can expand it through reading and research into various career areas.

Once you have specified your general work functions, break them down into sub-functions. For example, if you selected photography, how does the process break down? What particular aspects of the process seem more enjoyable? What specific functions do you think you have the best potential for performing?

Your analysis of several high interest and best potential areas can help you identify a few prime functions.

Your analysis of functions can provide you with criteria for what to look for as you evaluate various career opportunities. Handbooks such as *The Occupational Outlook Quarterly*, a government publication found in most public libraries, provide job specifications and current and future employment opportunities.

LEARNING THROUGH EXPERIMENTING

Your answer to a key question—do I have the talent, skill, and desire to function effectively on this job—can prove illuminating in assessing the viability of a career. Of course, you cannot always tell until you sample the job. But if you know what functions you like to perform and have an understanding of your potential to perform them, you already have a partial answer.

Sometimes experimentation provides surprise opportunities. Suppose you think you might like to work as a counselor. So you volunteer for a hot-line program and get training answering panic calls. In the process, you might discover that the hot line does not get enough publicity. So you volunteer to advertise the program and discover that you like advertising more than counseling. However, your counseling experience helps you to present your advertising ideas more effectively.

My own experience confirms the concept that "experience is the best teacher." For example, I know that I like to work with ideas, concepts, and people. Before I had ever written a book, I thought that writing would provide an opportunity to organize my thoughts on psychology and counseling, develop new mental health concepts, and add to my knowledge and expertise. I found that the process also allows me to involve myself in other exciting career options. I found that I like marketing the books by appearing on talk shows, giving public workshops, and developing ways to get the books in major bookstores.

My experiment in writing mainly allowed me to expand my primary vocational mission: disseminating psycho-educational information and concepts to help people develop their psychological competencies.

Although experimentation often proves valuable, you don't have to test out new experiences to know what you don't like.

Sometimes partial experiences give you enough data to make a decision. For example, I never traveled to the North Pole so I have not experienced the freezing temperatures there, but I have experienced cold weather so I know that I would not like that atmosphere.

RATIONAL CAREER MANAGEMENT

The exercises suggested in this chapter highlight the importance of self-evaluation through self-examination. They fit with what vocational counselors Elmer Kramer and James Hawkes have pointed out: self-improvement, self-evaluation, and achievement get linked in a chain that grows out of exploratory action plans.

In this section, I present a rational emotive therapy technique that can help strengthen the exploratory action chain. Rational emotive methods have traditionally found their niche in emotional problem-solving situations. They seem especially applicable to conditions where, as psychologist Walter Neff has pointed out, the person's personality problems interfere with work selection and adjustment. Some psychologically handicapped people, for example, feel afraid of work responsibilities and consequently don't really want to work. Under such conditions, gathering information through career-oriented tests, do-it-yourself methods, and advice will have questionable value. To benefit from vocational counseling, the person would best learn to overcome his or her psychological disturbance.

Psychological disturbances often grow from negative and unrealistic attitudes—faulty expectations, irrational ideas, misperceptions, and so forth. Unfortunately, as vocational test specialist Leo Goldman has noted, people often resist changing their self-defeating attitudes. And changing dysfunctional attitudes stands as a requisite for productive career counseling. If changes don't take place in core irrational attitudes, the person will have difficulty sorting out career options and realistically functioning in a career.

In addition to employing conventional career planning methods, the individual with dysfunctional career attitudes needs to learn to develop adaptive attitudes so that he can take better advantage of career guidance information. Rational emotive methods

can help reduce the impact of self-defeating attitudes and set the stage for productive career exploration.

The rational emotive method applies self-evaluation and rational action methods to cases where the person creates his or her own disturbances by faulty thinking. The method may have special value in instances where the person limits his vocational choices due to such factors as low frustration tolerance and discomfort-dodging, a poor self-concept, erroneous expectations, and procrastination.

Self-application of the rational emotive method in managing career frustrations requires some sophistication in the use of the method. The following material will get you started in the right direction. Books by William Knaus (1982), Albert Ellis, and Robert Harper (1975) can provide additional information on the practical use of the rational emotive method.

The rational emotive approach as described by Albert Ellis emphasizes reality-testing techniques people apply in learning to realistically understand themselves and their world. By learning to identify self-defeating attitudes and beliefs and actively disputing them, the person frees up his positive competencies for pursuing productive activities.

The rational emotive therapy system provides a model to help diminish or eliminate dysfunctional beliefs through rational self-examination methods. These methods include a DIBS technique, which stands for *D*isputing *I*rrational *B*elief *S*ystems. The method involves the process of stopping, focusing, and examining irrational beliefs that interfere with reality-testing capabilities. You *stop* and listen to what you tell yourself when you upset yourself. You *focus* on those thoughts so as to put them into perspective. Then you *examine* them by questioning the assumptions that support them. You can tell when you activate an irrational belief: when you act defensively or feel fearful, depressed, angry, or guilty. The irrational beliefs that support disturbed emotions usually include unrealistic but credible sounding demands such as: "I should not have hassles." Irrational beliefs also include low frustration tolerance words and phrases.

Common confusions exist in career planning and management that rational emotive questioning can help clear up. The following cites five common irrational thoughts that cause people difficulties and five rational-emotive-type (DIBS) questions that you can apply to each.

1. Common Vocational Hang-Ups Include Believing
   You should not have career frustrations.
   Vocational decisions should come easy.
   A perfect job exists.
   You don't deserve what you want.
   You can't possibly succeed, so why try?
2. Rational Questions to Counter Hang-Ups
   What evidence exists to support this belief?
   What evidence exists to counter this belief?
   What purpose does the belief serve?
   What stops me from countering questionable beliefs?
   How do I create and change my career frustrations?

Rational questioning also applies to situations where a person has adopted a polarizing all-or-nothing view about a career. Such a view may cause the person to take an unwarranted and extreme position. For example, the person who believes that unless he gets a college degree, he'll end up selling pencils for a living might profit by asking himself the five basic questions and then having a compassionate and trusted friend (or a counselor) evaluate his responses, support the rational ones, and dispute the irrational responses.

WHERE DO YOU GO FROM HERE?

If you feel unsettled or unhappy with your career choice, take stock of your interests, preferred functions, and abilities and see if you have some hidden aspirations you can actualize and hidden talents you can utilize. If your career seems headed in a good direction, see if you can't achieve more of what you want from your work.

If you want to get started on your career review but somehow keep putting it off, Chapter 9, Mastering Your Time Frustrations, addresses that issue.

CHAPTER NINE

MASTERING YOUR TIME FRUSTRATIONS

How often have you heard people say that they work better under pressure? You may have said this yourself. If you have, welcome to the club—the procrastinators' club.

"Me, a procrastinator?" you might say. "Well, maybe sometimes. But I don't see how working better under pressure has anything to do with putting things off."

Think a minute. What does working better under pressure mean to you? Although not universally true, "working better under pressure" often turns out to mean that we've put something off and now find ourselves rushed to meet a deadline.

Why would anyone work better under pressure? Why would anyone want to, for that matter, when he can implement ways to act effectively and have time to get things done? Indeed, why would anyone put himself in a position where he had to rush to get a job done?

In this chapter we will look into some of the symptoms of procrastination and its causes and solutions. We will look into ways to turn this habit pattern off and turn on a less pressured and more productive and pleasurable style of living.

A CLASSIC PROCRASTINATOR

George breathlessly arrived at the airline ticket counter to buy a ticket just moments before the flight's scheduled departure. The clerk behind the ticket counter told him that flights fill up weeks in advance during peak travel holiday periods. If he had expected to get a flight during the Christmas rush, he would have had to make reservations long in advance.

Prior to leaving for the airport, George had felt frustrated when he couldn't locate critical items he needed for the trip. In addition, he realized too late that he had forgotten to get his car inspected and his old sticker was out of date. As he rushed out the door, he saw the pile of trash waiting to get thrown out and the application to graduate school he still had to fill out.

Like many people, George has a habit of putting things off until the last minute. His friends have joked that he will probably show up late to his own funeral. However, the problem does not seem very funny to George. So, particularly discouraged with the frustrating events of the day, he vowed that he would take charge of his life and do something positive to stop his procrastination problem, beginning now!

THE PROCRASTINATION HANG-UP

We all put things off from time to time, and our procrastination acts often do no more than hinder, frustrate, and annoy us. However, procrastination can develop into an emotional hang-up that can have self-defeating outcomes. The self-sabotaging effects of this habit can ruin careers, create serious interpersonal discord, and promote emotional misery and suffering.

In the remainder of this chapter we will take a close look at why people put things off. As we do, we will consider how to eliminate this pattern and add years of *productive* time to our lives. We will look at what procrastination means and what we can do to control this habit in the following nine sections:

1. Procrastination defined
2. Everyday procrastination
3. Time-thief delays

4. Maintenance and development procrastination
5. The paradox
6. The complications
7. The cover-up
8. Facing the problem
9. Moving forward

PROCRASTINATION DEFINED

Procrastination refers to needlessly putting off, postponing, or delaying a timely and relevant activity. This universal problem represents a conscious or semiconscious *choice* to needlessly delay action. It can occur at any stage of a project—conceiving, planning, initiating, processing, and completing.

Although we can define procrastination as putting off anything we choose to do, this definition unless clarified has flaws. For example, we may legitimately lag in doing certain things because we lack information, have skill deficiencies, forget, schedule or design delays into our work, feel ill or fatigued. Although some of these reasons for procrastination have some legitimacy—lacking information and skill deficiencies—putting off corrective action constitutes procrastination.

EVERYDAY PROCRASTINATION

We see many examples of procrastination in everyday life:

1. You decide you'll diet *after* the holidays.
2. You swear you'll give up smoking *someday*.
3. You repeatedly show up late for appointments or breathlessly arrive at the eleventh hour feeling rushed.
4. You think school homework assignments can wait until tomorrow's study hall.
5. You want to write the Great American Novel but can't seem to get started. You wait for inspiration.
6. You have a debilitating fear of strangers and panic at the thought of meeting new people.
7. You have a long list of things to do around the house that don't seem to get done. You tell yourself that you don't have the time or you say that dealing with details clutters your busy life.

121

8. You tell yourself that you'll get that extra education you've always wanted one of these days.
9. You fear making an appointment for a medical examination or dental work and substitute worrying for action.
10. You lack self-confidence but don't act to build your confidence.

Of course we could easily add to the preceding list. Who doesn't, from time to time, procrastinate? Even well-known people do it. The billionaire Howard Hughes put off dealing with his agoraphobic problem. Ex-President Jimmy Carter reputedly had his disorganized files shipped to Plains, Georgia, shortly before the Reagans moved into the White House.

The decision makers of major corporations sometimes procrastinate (or we find them "asleep at the wheel"). For example, long after video games had caught fire, a representative of a major toy manufacturer stated that the company viewed video games as a passing fad and wouldn't produce them. One year later, the company belatedly got into the video game market.

Managers of major league sports clubs have also been caught procrastinating. For example, in 1981 the Boston Red Sox home office forgot to send their star catcher Carlton Fisk his contract and ended up paying a penalty for their oversight.

Sometimes we have to pay for our procrastinating. Public and governmental agencies have come to expect people to procrastinate. Libraries fine for late book returns. Interest penalties for late tax returns provide the government with a tidy profit. Municipal governments collect late penalty fees for traffic violations. The telephone company disconnects service and charges a reconnection fee for those customers not paying their bills on time.

Public complaints of bureaucratic procrastination would fill the New York City library. Such inefficiencies, whether you call them procrastination or not, often prove frustrating.

Of course, students procrastinate. Various studies have shown that at least twenty-five percent of college students routinely procrastinate on their assignments. The others procrastinate less regularly. Considering the personal and dollar cost of a college education, procrastination constitutes a major academic waste of time.

When we follow procrastination practices, we develop a tolerance for this behavior and pay an emotional and dollar price for that tolerance. Fortunately, we can build our procrastination awareness, go on a procrastination alert, and take action to overcome the problem.

TIME-THIEF DELAYS

We have many subtle ways of causing ourselves delays: daydreaming, mindlessly smoking or drinking coffee, habitual grooming or fingernail filing, worry, fretting over our unwanted emotions, giving up too easily, creating crises, puttering around, compulsive socializing, reading trite and insipid material, excessive television watching, dawdling, shuffling papers, unnecessarily rechecking work, excessively using drugs or alcohol, dragging out a project by com-

plaining about how onerous we find it, and so forth. These all represent *time-thief* activities.

One of the worst time-thief pranks, the "paper shuffle," often consumes considerable time: opening and reading junk mail, handling the same paperwork two or three times, letting your files or desk pile up so you have to sort through all your papers.

Interruptions constitute another major source of time loss as well as frustration. We don't need many examples to expose such time-thief episodes. Interruptions, however, don't just come from other people. We often interrupt ourselves. For example, we interrupt ourselves when we dwell upon incomplete projects, such as the messy garage, the unanswered phone call, and the basket of dirty laundry. These tasks can take an outstanding position in perception, memory, and thinking and distract us from focusing upon our main priorities. Ridding yourself of internal interruptions lies, in part, with completing the incomplete tasks that nag on your mind.

Recurrent external or internal interruptions can prove so frustrating that the person procrastinates by stewing over the interruption.

To beat the time thief it makes little sense to try to function like a robot at 100 percent efficiency. You would soon burn out. Instead, build elasticity into your schedule by including time for thinking, planning, winding down, communicating ideas, receiving feedback, relaxing, and personal development. To make time for these activities, monitor your activities to identify time-waste practices and make action changes designed to shrink the waste.

For example, if your time study reveals that you start your day by putting your preparation priorities on the back burner as you fritter away time in busy work, reverse the pattern. Gather your things the night before. In the morning, shower, dress, and then do the busy work until the time to leave. Such changes may cause you to lose out on the challenge of playing "beat the clock," but it will pay off in a more relaxed pace and in getting to places on time.

MAINTENANCE AND DEVELOPMENT PROCRASTINATION

People procrastinate both in maintaining their environments and in developing their skills, competencies, and opportunities.

Maintenance procrastination refers to putting off daily details such as shopping for groceries, paying bills, or keeping our homes in good order.

Development procrastination refers to putting off, delaying, or postponing activities such as taking classes to promote personal growth and to open up opportunities.

THE PARADOX

Procrastination patterns can lead to chronic frustration, disturbance, and even health problems. A habitual procrastination pattern almost certainly limits career progress, the quality of interpersonal relationships, and recreational opportunities.

In contrast constructive actions can have a positive payoff. For example, when we get things done on schedule, when we don't feel swamped by incomplete tasks, and when we act in an organized and responsible manner, we tend to think clearly, have greater command over the direction of our lives, and feel more productive and capable. In addition we have more time to do the things we enjoy doing and feel more relaxed about doing them.

Why then do people put off timely actions and replace them with avoidance actions that have potentially onerous consequences? Let's look into some of these reasons.

Sometimes people put things off because they don't think they deserve to succeed. Some people fear the responsibilities of success. Some hate to feel inconvenienced or uncomfortable, so they procrastinate to dodge discomfort. Perfectionists dare not act until they feel confident that their actions will prove unassailable, or perfect. Still others put off because of rebelliousness. Some procrastinate because they have a poor self-concept and fear exposing their weaknesses. Others do so because of a poor sense of timing and pacing: they underestimate the time it will take to prepare and to perform. We may put off something when we view the task as overwhelming or highly unpleasant, especially if we think it will prove time-consuming. We also may procrastinate on preliminary steps we know we can take easily, because such actions may cause us to work at something later that we may not want to take the time to do.

Of course we could easily add to the list of what motivates procrastination. We also can adapt the concept of inertia from the work of the nineteenth-century physicist Isaac Newton to understand why people continue to put things off. According to Newton, a body at rest tends to stay at rest, and a body in motion tends to stay in motion. Applied to procrastination, the principle works as follows: if you procrastinate, you will find it easier to continue to procrastinate than to shift into action. *It takes a willful and intentional effort to start yourself moving.* But once you get started, you'll find it easier to continue than to stop.

We can consolidate most of the above dynamics into a play-off between self-doubts and discomfort-dodging. In the following section, we'll look into procrastination complications as a prelude to the question: If we don't like the results, why play the game?

THE COMPLICATIONS

Researchers who study the procrastination problem quickly learn that procrastination serves many functions. For example, procrastination has the qualities of a symptom, a defense, and a problem habit. Frequently, all three conditions coexist and cause a network of complications.

1. As a symptom, procrastination can reflect debilitating self-doubts, serious low frustration tolerance, and accompanying discomfort-dodging activities.
2. As a defense, procrastination can reflect a fear of failure and therefore serves as a diversion from facing that fear.
3. As a problem habit, procrastination can reflect irresponsibility, poor self-discipline, and/or poor organizing skills. It can also represent a problem of complacency, indifference, or inertia.

Although each procrastinator shares the common problem of putting things off, procrastination can appear like a collage of motivations.

THE COVER-UP

People who procrastinate often refine excuse making to a well-practiced art. They invent face-saving excuses when they think about putting things off. However, although often temporarily palliative, in the long run these cover-ups backfire, leaving the procrastinator with feelings of distress, inadequacy, and frustration as a by-product of thoughtlessly choosing comfort over change.

Procrastination excuses usually fall into mañana, contingency mañana, and "catch 22" categories.

The *mañana* excuse happens when you tell yourself that you'll do something tomorrow that you could do today, such as paying the bills or raking the leaves. One client said that in the "next" life he will profit from the mistakes of this life and not procrastinate!

In the *contingency mañana* excuse, you fixate on a problem that appears to relate to your primary problem. Then you make dealing successfully with that peripheral problem the prerequisite for tackling your primary problem. For example, you promise yourself that you will make new friends. But you think you weigh too much and don't know enough about world events to appeal to others. So you swear you'll lose weight and get up to date on world events. Then you put off starting your weight-reduction program (or don't stick to the one you've started) and distract yourself from reading about world events. You aggravate yourself about your lack of progress and conveniently forget about facing your fear of meeting people.

In *catch 22* you convince yourself that no way exists to get out of your presumably impossible situation. For example, you tell yourself you don't have the brain power to learn the job of your dreams and no other job will do. When you harbor this attitude, you have locked yourself into a no-change position, and you likely will continue to procrastinate on finding satisfying employment until you radically modify this self-defeating and inhibitory attitude.

Each cover-up excuse has as a common factor a decision—the task will get done later or seems impossible so why try. Such excuses can bring temporary relief, because either some day the task will get done or, since one can't succeed, why worry. Of course, no guarantee exists that one will feel more like taking action later.

We orchestrate our procrastination experiences when we "wheedle" ourselves into doing a hesitation waltz. By agreeing with our procrastination excuse, we make the wrong decision and fall into the postponement trap. The Wheedler presents an example of the oxymorin (two opposites together, such as kindness-cruelness) that represents procrastination.

FACING THE PROBLEM

People often commit themselves to the *idea* of change, but not to the *effort* of change. As a result, they fail to properly assess their situation, to carefully identify achievable goals, to formulate plans, to organize for action, and to put the plans into action. Instead, they have the erroneous idea that change should come easily, and that minor efforts will result in major achievements. Such thinking constitutes an unrealistic posturing for facing an enigmatic problem that proves resistive to change.

The extent of your progress in overcoming this pattern depends upon the rigor and persistence with which you apply your efforts. Success depends upon how strongly you *intend* to work to develop your constructive capabilities.

The process of developing constructive capabilities has an evolutionary quality. As you practice acting effectively, you get better at it. The tougher you get on the problem, the kinder you act toward yourself. When you creatively and pragmatically work to master your frustrations by overcoming procrastination, you reduce the amount of distress and disturbance in your life and liberate your mind to concentrate on present and future challenges, instead of stewing about the past and worrying about the future. In this challenging process, the more skills you develop, the more tolerant you'll feel about your periodic lapses. They will serve an important function of highlighting your normal human imperfections; provide you with opportunities to learn self-tolerance; provide review opportunities where you can practice taking corrective actions. After all, no reasonable person expects us to act superhuman.

In our change efforts it makes sense to *accept* such shortcomings as they exist in ourselves and act to correct them.

Success will not come simply by gaining intellectual understanding; you have to act your way out. Perhaps you may integrate new learnings in that process, accept your limitations, and understand your potentials. If you never try, you'll never win.

The following represents a ten-step stall-stopper program:

1. Make a commitment to develop skill in managing your time and talents, using the psychological and time-management strategies presented here to help you.
2. Recognize that it will take good planning, responsive management, and effort to develop an effective time-management system.
3. Establish clear and achievable goals. Avoid toying with unachievable goals—those you can't clearly define or measure, or that don't fit with your interests, temperament, or abilities.
4. Get clear on your priorities and get to work. Make a point to work on your top priorities before beginning the lesser ones. Avoid substituting trivial activities, such as pruning hedges, for important proj-

ects, such as preparing for an examination. But don't act inflexibly. Sometimes you can quickly throw off minor priorities in spare moments.

Specify your priorities according to long term, monthly, and daily. Write down your daily and monthly priorities, list them according to importance, and color code them according to importance. For example, code red = top priority, blue = important, green = do after everything else gets done. Cross them out after you complete them. Repeat this practice daily.

5. In your career planning, on a monthly basis block off time for planned meetings, conferences, and red projects. Then fill your time schedule with blue priorities, then green priorities.

Plan your time so that you have opportunities to develop skills, build quality into your work, relax, and still meet flexible and realistic schedules and deadlines. Keep the schedule loose enough to allow time for the unexpected, for underestimating the time necessary to complete the project, and for winding down.

In your spare time create time for exercise, mental development, and fun. If you have a family, try to get them involved in creative and fun ways to use their time, and try to learn from them as they learn with you.

6. Identify where your procrastination starts. Do you bog down at the stage of inception when you first decide what you will do? Do you snare yourself when you first start to make plans? Do you set up your plans and organization then fizzle out? Do you start but fade in the stretch? Do you complete your major projects on time then hand them in late? If so, then see what you can do to change the pattern.

7. Determine how you stop yourself from acting effectively and productively. Do you thoughtlessly dodge discomfort? Do you use too much time doubting your abilities to the extent that you second-guess yourself, hesitate, and wait for a guarantee that you will do well? Do you have vague goals and objectives? Once you have diagnosed the problem, determine what you can do to start to break the pattern and forge a new and effective pattern—starting *now*.

8. Get organized, especially with the everyday stuff. Manage the easily put off daily routines, such as washing clothes, shopping for groceries or presents, preparing for special events, returning phone calls, and writing letters. Keep in mind that the little things can frustrate and trap you. Sometimes the accumulation of minor matters culminates in strong feelings of anxiety that can have a disorganizing effect on performance and put you farther behind.

9. Break it down. Use a bits-and-pieces approach as part of your organizing plan. Break your major projects down into realistically manageable steps.

10. Get started. Use the *five-minute* plan. Decide that you will start off by putting five minutes into your project, and at the end of five minutes

you will decide if you will continue for another five minutes. You can use this action step to help yourself break patterns of inertia. Start to use this five-minute plan to dispense with routine daily matters and time-consuming complex problems as soon as you recognize them.

The five-minute plan has many adaptations. You can use it in any phase of your project when you start to procrastinate. You can also use it as a tool to help you break an unwanted habit. For example, if you want to stop binging on fattening goodies, try to avoid the binge habit for five minutes when you first feel the urge to gorge. At the end of that five-minute time period, decide if you will resist the urge for the next five minutes. You continue with this five-minute process until you overcome your low frustration tolerance urges and break the habit.

MOVING FORWARD

In an atmosphere of change where we shun procrastination and substitute more efficient actions, the person pioneering his or her psychological actualization works within a framework in which frustration, stress, and disappointment share the same space with revelation, discovery, and joy. To reap the benefits of revelation and to experience the feeling of the joy of discovery requires that one commit to the goal of acceptance of one's natural ambivalence (fears and curiosity) about both the known and the unexplored waters of knowledge and *invest* the time necessary to discover and master those unfamiliar but personally worthwhile and potentially gratifying areas. To embark on this course of change, it helps to resist predicting that the effort that looms ahead will prove too uncomfortable to justify itself. Instead, look to the future as a challenge that provides many growth opportunities.

Move forward. Don't shy away from facing the inevitable "good" frustrations that might result from your efforts. In this pursuit, risk exposing your ignorances and deficiencies in order to overcome them and to discover constructive qualities and talents. In this quest, take the risk that your talents and capabilities may not evolve into great skills and competencies. Know that your frustrations will continue to accompany you even as you gain mastery.

Those who embark upon this uncertain journey eventually learn to give as much care and effort to their own development as they would a garden they chose to care for, and to help themselves as they would help the living plants grow stronger and more fruitful.

In the end, what we do gets done by living through frustrations, struggle, and strain without the assurances of success.

BIBLIOGRAPHY

The following references refer to materials cited in this work. Some of these references may prove helpful to the person interested in learning more about cognitive behavior self-help strategies. I've marked such works with an asterisk.

Aesop's fables, New York: Avenel, a facsimile of the 1912 edition.

Ainslie, G. "Specious reward: A behavior theory of impulsiveness and impulse control," *Psychological Bulletin*, 1975, *82*, 463–496.

Allport, G. W. *Becoming*, New Haven: Yale University Press, 1955.

Allport, G. W. *Pattern and growth in personality*, New York: Holt, Rinehart & Winston, 1937.

Belloc, N. D. "Relationship of health practices and mortality," *Preventative Medicine*, 1973, *2*, 67–81.

Bem, D. J. "Self-perception: an alternative interpretation of the cognitive dissonance phenomenon," *Psychological Review*, 1967, *74*, 183–200.

Berkowitz, L. "Control of aggression," in B. M. Caldwell & H. Ricciuti (Eds.), *Review of Child Development Research*, Vol. 3, 1969.

Birch, H. G. & Rabinowitz, H. S. "The negative effects of previous experience on productive thinking," *Journal of Experimental Psychology*, 1951, *41*, 121–125.

Birch, H. G. "The relationship of previous experience to insightful problem solving," *Journal of Comparative Psychology*, 1945, *38*, 367–383.

Bolles, R. N. *What color is your parachute?*, Berkeley, Calif.: Ten Speed Press, 1977.

Boring, E. G. *A history of experimental psychology*, New York: Appleton-Century-Crofts, 1950.

Bourland, D. D. "A linguistic note: Writing in E-prime," *General Semantics Bulletin*, 1965–1966, *32–33*, 111–114.

Bull, N. "Emotion as frustrational behavior," *Journal of Nervous and Mental Disease*, 1957, *125*, 4, 622–628.

Campbell, J. *The hero of a thousand faces*, Princeton, N.J.: Princeton University Press, 1968.

Carver, C. S., & Scheier, M. F. "Control theory: A useful conceptual framework for personal, social, clinical, and health psychology," *Psychological Bulletin*, 1982, *92*, *1*, 111–135.

Cattell, R. "Advances in the measurement of neuroticism and anxiety in a conceptual framework of unitary-trait theory," *Annals of the New York Academy of Sciences*, 1962, *93*, *20*, 813–856.

Cherry, E. C. *On human communication*, Cambridge, Mass.: M.I.T. Press, 1965.

Diagnostic and statistical manual of mental disorders (DSM III), 3rd. ed., Washington, D.C., 1980.

Dollard, J., Doob, L., Miller, N., Mowrer, O. H., & Sears, R. *Frustration and aggression*, New Haven: Yale University Press, 1939.

Duncker, K. "On problem solving," *Psychological Monographs*, 1945, *58*, No. *270*.

*Ellis, A. *Reason and emotion in psychotherapy*, New York: Lyle Stuart, 1962.

*Ellis, A. "Disputing irrational belief systems," Leaflet, New York: Institute for Rational Emotive Psychotherapy, 1975.

*Ellis, A. *How to live with and without anger*, Pleasantville, N.Y.: Reader's Digest Press, 1977.

*Ellis, A., & Harper, R. A. *A new guide to rational living*, Englewood Cliffs, N.J.: Prentice-Hall, 1975.

*Ellis, A., & Knaus, W. *Overcoming procrastination*, New York: New American Library, 1979.

Friedman, M., & Rosenman, R. *Type A behavior and your heart*, Greenwich, Conn.: Fawcett Crest, 1974.

Fromm, E. *The art of loving*, New York: Harper & Row, 1974.

Gaiennie, L. R. "Strategies for career management," Unpublished paper, University of Southern Florida, 1981.

Glasser, M. L., & Glass, G. V. "Meta analysis of psychotherapy outcome studies," *American Psychologist*, 1977, *32*, *9*, 752–760.

Glasser W. *Mental health or mental illness*, New York: Harper & Row, 1970.

Goethe, J. W. *Faust*, New York: Norton, 1976.

Goldman, L. *Using tests in counseling* (2nd ed.), New York: Appleton-Century-Crofts, 1971.

Grimm's fairy tales, New York: Avenel, 1981.

Hammerlie, F. M., & Montgomery, R. L. "Self-perception theory and unobstrusively biased interactions: A treatment for homosexual anxiety," *Journal of Counseling Psychology*, 1982, *29*, *4*, 362–370.

Hartshorne, H., & May, M. "Studies in deceit," in *Studies in the nature of character*, New York: Macmillan, Vol. 1, 1928–1930.

Heron, W. "Cognitive and physiological effects of perceptual isolation," in P. Solomon, et al (Eds.), *Sensory deprivation*, Cambridge, Mass.: Harvard University Press, 1961.

Hoffer, E. *The true believer*, New York: Harper & Row, 1951.

Hogan, R. "Moral conduct and moral character: a psychological perspective," *Psychological Bulletin*, 1975, *79*, *4*, 217–232.

Holms, T., & Rahe, R. "The social re-adjustment rating scale," *Psychosomatic Research*, 1967, *11*, 213–218.

Homer, *The odyssey*, Garden City, N.Y.: Doubleday, 1961.

James, W. *Psychology*, New York: Holt, 1892.

*Knaus, W. "Overcoming procrastination," *Rational Living*, 1973, *8*, 2–7.

*Knaus, W. *Do it now: how to stop procrastination*, Englewood Cliffs, N.J.: Prentice-Hall, 1979.

*Knaus, W. *How to get out of a rut*, Englewood Cliffs, N.J.: Prentice-Hall, 1982.

*Knaus, W. "Children and low frustration tolerance," in A. Ellis & M. Bernard (Eds.), *Rational-emotive approaches to the problems of childhood*, New York: Plenum, 1984.

Kohlberg, L. "Stage and sequence: The cognitive developmental approach to socialization," in D. Goslin (Ed.), *Handbook of Socialization Theory and Research*, New York: Rand McNally, 1969.

Korzybski, A. *Science and sanity* (4th ed.), Lakewood, Conn.: International Non-Aristotelian Library, 1958.

Kramer, E. E., & Hawkes, J. P. *Reality coping and employment adjustment*, Ft. Collins, Colo.: Colorado State University, 1968.

Kuhn, T. *The structure of scientific revolutions*, Chicago: University of Chicago Press (2nd enlarged ed.), 1970.

Levenkron, J. C., Cohen, J. D., Mueller, H., & Fisher, E. B. "Modifying the Type A coronary prone behavior pattern," *Journal of Consulting and Clinical Psychology*, 1983, *51*, 2, 192–204.

Lewin, K. *A dynamic theory of personality*, New York: McGraw-Hill, 1935.

Lewin, K., Lippitt, R., & White, R. K. "Patterns of aggressive behavior in experimentally created social climates," *Journal of Social Psychology*, 1939, *10*, 271–299.

Low, A. A. *Mental health through will training*, Boston: Christopher Publishing, 1950.

Luborsky, L., Singer, B., & Luborsky, L. "Comparative studies of psychotherapies," *Archives of General Psychiatry*, 1975, *32*, 995–1008.

Q

R

responsibility and, 83
  situational variables and, 76
Vocational bootstrap programs,
  108
Vocations, *See* Careers.

W

Washington, George, 1
Weight control, *See* Eating
  behaviors.

Whisper technique, 56–57
Whitman, Walt, 81
Woodworth, Robert S., 7
Work, *See* Careers.
Work-a-holism, 52, 54
Worry and disapproval fears, 38

Z

Zeitgeist, 63–64

Luria, A. R. *The role of speech in the regulation of normal and abnormal behavior*, New York: Livermore, 1961.

Maier, N.R.F. "Experimentally induced abnormal behavior," *The Scientific Monthly*, September 1948, 210–216.

Maier, N.R.F. "Reasoning in humans: The mechanisms of equivalent stimuli and of reasoning," *Journal of Experimental Psychology*, 1954, *35*, 349–360.

McDougal, W. "Purposive or mechanical psychology?", *Psychological Review*, 1923, *30*, 273–288.

*Meichenbaum, D. H. "Self-instructional methods," in F. H. Kanfer and A. D. Goldstein (Eds.), *Helping people change: A textbook of methods*, New York: Pergamon, 1975.

*Meichenbaum, D. H. & Goodman, J. "Training impulsive children to talk to themselves," *Journal of Abnormal Psychology*, 1971, *77*, 115–126.

Minski, M. (Ed.), *Semantic information processing*, Cambridge, Mass.: M.I.T. Press, 1968.

Neff, W. *Work and human behavior*, New York: Atherton, 1968.

Occupational outlook handbook, 1982–1983 Ed., U.S. Dept. of Labor.

Perls, F., Hefferline, R., & Goodman, P. *Gestalt therapy*, New York: Julian Press, 1951.

Peter, L. *The Peter principle*, Sun City, Fla.: Hull, 1970.

Piaget, J. *The psychology of the child*, New York: Basic Books, 1969.

Prentice, W.C.H., "Some cognitive aspects of motivation," *American Psychologist*, 1961, *16*, 503–511.

Raths, L. E., Harmin, M., & Simon, S. B. *Values and teaching*, Columbus, Ohio: Merrill, 1966.

Raush, H. L, Barry, W. A., Hertel, R. K., & Swain, M. A. *Communication, conflict, and marriage*, San Francisco: Jossey-Bass, 1974.

*Schachter, S. "Recidivism and self-cure of smoking and obesity," *American Psychologist*, 1982, *37*, 4, 436–444.

*Schachter, S., & Singer, J. E. "Cognitive, social, and physiological determinants of emotional state," *Psychological Review*, 1962, *69*, 397–399.

Selye, H. *Stress without distress*, New York: Signet, 1975.

Swift, J. *Gulliver's travels*, 13th printing, New York: Rinehart, 1958.

Terkel, S. *Working*, New York: Pantheon, 1972.

Thorndike, E. L. *Human learning*, New York: Appleton-Century-Crofts, 1931.

Toynbee, A. *War and civilization*, New York: Oxford University Press, 1950.

Webster's seventh new collegiate dictionary, Springfield, Mass.: G. & C. Merriam Co., 1972.

Whitman, W. *Leaves of grass*, Ithaca, N.Y.: Cornell University Press, 1961.

*Wolpe, J. "Behavior therapy in complex neurotic states," *British Journal of Psychiatry*, 1964, *110*, 28–34.

Woodworth, R. S. *Experimental psychology*, New York: Holt, 1938.